Business
Advantage

Personal Study Book
Upper-intermediate

Joy Godwin

CAMBRIDGE
UNIVERSITY PRESS

CAMBRIDGE
UNIVERSITY PRESS

University Printing House, Cambridge CB2 8BS, United Kingdom

One Liberty Plaza, 20th Floor, New York, NY 10006, USA

477 Williamstown Road, Port Melbourne, VIC 3207, Australia

4843/24, 2nd Floor, Ansari Road, Daryaganj, Delhi – 110002, India

79 Anson Road, #06–04/06, Singapore 079906

Cambridge University Press is part of the University of Cambridge.

It furthers the University's mission by disseminating knowledge in the pursuit of
education, learning and research at the highest international levels of excellence.

www.cambridge.org
Information on this title: www.cambridge.org/9780521281300

© Cambridge University Press 2011

First published 2011
20 19 18 17 16 15 14 13 12 11 10 9 8 7 6

Printed in Great Britain by CPI Group (UK) Ltd, Croydon CR0 4YY

A catalogue record for this publication is available from the British Library

ISBN 978-0-521-13217-6 Upper-intermediate Student's Book with DVD
ISBN 978-1-107-42231-5 Upper-intermediate Teacher's Book
ISBN 978-0-521-28130-0 Upper-intermediate Personal Study Book with Audio CD
ISBN 978-0-521-13218-3 Upper-intermediate Audio CDs

Contents

Introduction to the Personal Study Book   4

1 Competitive environment   5–7
2 Future uncertainty   8–10

Reading 1: Food Retail in India   11–12
Writing 1: Preparing presentation slides   13

3 Rewarding performance   14–16
4 Fostering creativity   17–19

Reading 2: Entrepreneurship: two schools of thought   20–21
Writing 2: Describing a process   22

5 Organisational cultures   23–25
6 Working across cultures   26–28

Reading 3: Geert Hofstede   29–30
Writing 3: Argument-led writing   31

7 Change management   32–34
8 Project management   35–37

Reading 4: Peter Drucker and his talent to spot trends   38–39
Writing 4: Describing graphs   40

9 E-marketing   41–43
10 Branding   44–46

Reading 5: The power of words   47–48
Writing 5: Persuasive communication online   49

11 Accounting   50–52
12 Microfinance   53–55

Reading 6: Microfinance for small business owners   56–57
Writing 6: Formal and informal emails at work   58

13 Corporate Social Responsibility   59–61
14 Strategic planning   62–64

Reading 7: Henry Mintzberg   65–66
Writing 7: First contact emails   67

Wordlist   68–71

Grammar reference   72–77

Progress tests   78–83

Audio scripts   84–86

Answer key   87–95

Acknowledgements   96

Introduction

What's in this book?

This book is designed to help you test the grammar, vocabulary and skills you have learnt through studying *Business Advantage Upper-intermediate by Michael Handford, Martin Lisboa, Almut Koester and Angela Pitt*. There are 14 units, one for each unit of the book. In addition, there are seven Writing sections, each matching the relevant writing section of the book. There are also seven Reading sections related to the topics covered in the Student's Book. Each unit follows the Student's Book closely: there is a section related to each of the three lessons in each unit of the Student's Book. You will find an Answer key at the back of the book.

There are also three progress tests: one after Units 1–5, another one after Units 6–10 and the last one after Units 11–14. You can use these to check your progress.

How do I use this book?

There are five stages in preparing for and using the units.

- *Preparation*: Study a unit or lesson of the Student's Book thoroughly. When you feel confident that you have mastered *all* the key words, grammar and skills presented, you are ready to complete the relevant section or unit of the Personal Study Book (PSB).
- *Practice*: Each unit contains two sections – grammar/vocabulary and skills. These relate directly to the material in the Student's Book. There are exercises in the skills section which include listening material: this gives you the opportunity to hear and practise key phrases and pronunciation, intonation and stress related to the skill you have learned in the Student's Book. Try to do all the questions in the section: each exercise tests one area of vocabulary, grammar or group of expressions from a skill area.
- *Checking*: When you have finished all the tasks, check your work. Then use the Answer key at the back of the book to mark your work. If you have made a lot of mistakes with one part, go back and check the Student's Book: review the key points to make sure you understand them.
- *Can Do statements*: At the end of each unit, there are two to three statements which give you an indication of what you should be able to do after completing the unit. There are two boxes next to each statement (*Yes, I can do this / I think I need more practice*). If you can answer 'Yes' to all the statements and you have got most of the exercises correct, then you are ready to move on to the next unit. If not, refer back to the relevant unit of the Student's Book.

- *Revision*: After completing the statements think about the areas you could work on in the furure and how you can do this. For example, if you think you need to do more work on an area of vocabulary, think about how you can do this and make a note of it. It is important to be realistic when you are studying – take one area at a time and don't try to do too much. It is better to learn five to six new items of vocabulary really thoroughly than try to remember more words which you will not be able to use effectively.

Reading and Writing Sections

There is a Reading section and a Writing section after each two units of the PSB. The reading topics look at the gurus behind the theories and other companies related to the companies you have studied in the Student's Book. All the reading texts are based on authentic materials and will probably contain some unknown words. There are some explanations and exercises to help you understand these, so do not worry if you do not understand every word the first time you read the text. If you find some interesting new vocabulary in the text, make a note of it and try to use it in order to help you remember it.

The writing units match the topics covered in the writing units of the Student's Book. There are some exercises to practise different aspects and types of writing and each unit ends with a longer piece of writing for you to complete. There is no Answer key for this final activity. When you have done the writing, ask your teacher or a native speaker to check it for you if possible. If this is not possible, read your work through critically and try to make any corrections. Remember, writing (even in your own language) is a process, with several stages: it is unusual to write something important without making changes before you complete it.

I hope this book will support you while you improve your business English and that the exercises will help you remember and practise the important vocabulary, grammar and skills that you will need in your work.

I hope you enjoy using the book and good luck with your English!

Joy Godwin

Joy Godwin

Acknowledgements for Business Advantage Upper-intermediate Personal Study Book

The author would like to thank Chris Capper and Neil Holloway at Cambridge for their guidance and input, Alison Bewsher for her editorial support and Michael Handford, Martin Lisboa, Almut Koester and Angela Pitt for providing the original material on which the exercises are based.

1 Competitive environment

Vocabulary and Grammar

Sport as a metaphor for business

1 Match each business term to its definition.

1	oligopoly	a	it is more efficient for one firm to serve an entire market than two or more, e.g. water distribution
2	perfect competition	b	a situation where a few firms dominate the market, e.g. the soft drinks market in the UK
3	business environment	c	a set of forces (political, economic, social, technical) which are mainly outside the control of a business and can have an impact on it
4	natural monopoly	d	a company which dominates and controls a specific industry
5	monopoly	e	a market condition where no buyer or seller has the economic power to fix the price of a product or service

2 Complete the sentences by choosing the correct alternative from the words in brackets.

1 What is the future of agriculture and the food sector in an increasingly _____ world? (competition / globalised / monopolised)

2 _____ competition is characterised by many buyers and sellers, many products that are similar in nature and, as a result, many substitutes. (Perfect / Natural / Business)

3 The insurance sector in India was _____ monopolised by state-run enterprises until 1999. (increasingly / naturally / largely)

4 In this talk, we will explore the challenges and opportunities managers face in the current business _____ . (environment / competition / monopoly)

5 Despite successive reviews by the Government and Ofcom, ITV remains one of Britain's most _____ regulated businesses. (largely / heavily / increasingly)

6 Some regulation of a _____ monopoly may be necessary to protect their captive customers. (natural / globalised / largely)

Adjective and adjective + noun combinations

1 Complete the sentences using the correct form of the words in brackets.

1 In 1665, Louis XIV granted patents to establish 26 glass manufacturers: his main _____ and _____ agenda was to undermine the Venetians' supremacy in the glassmaking industry. (politics, economics)

2 In 1684, St Gobain received an _____ and _____ order: mirrors for the Palace of Versailles. (impress, symbol)

3 After the French Revolution, the company lost their _____ and technical monopoly in the European glass market. (law)

4 Between 1986 and 1996, St Gobain worked to restore _____ and _____ growth. (sustain, profit)

2 One word is wrong in each of the sentences below. <u>Underline</u> the mistake and write the correct word at the end of the sentence.

1 Many people would like to see control of the banking system on the politics agenda. _____

2 The economical agenda will lead to a cut in welfare payments. _____

3 McAlpine have received an impressing order to build the office blocks. _____

4 Tel Mex lost its legality monopoly and several competitors were able to enter the market. _____

5 The public are still not spending so it is unlikely we will see a period of sustaining growth. _____

Tenses that talk about the past

1 Read the history of Carrefour, the French supermarket group, and use the correct form of the verbs from the box below to complete the text.

merge	open	expand	announce	take over	sell
set up	diversify	launch	reduce		

1959	The Fournier and Defforey families 1 _____ the Carrefour company.
1973–1975	The company 2 _____ its first hypermarkets in Spain and Brazil.
1984	The company 3 _____ into insurance services.
1989	The company opened its first Asian supermarket, in Taiwan.
1991	The company 4 _____ Euromarche and Montlaur companies.
1990s	The company 5 _____ into China.
1999	Carrefour and Promodes 6 _____ to create the largest European food retail group.
2000	The company 7 _____ its online supermarket, ooshop.
2005	The company 8 _____ 15 hypermarkets in Slovakia and the Czech Republic to Tesco.
2008	The company 9 _____ overall energy consumption by 13.6%.
2009	The company 10 _____ total sales of €96.2 billion.
2010	159th hypermarket opened in China

2 Complete the sentences using the correct tense of the verb in brackets.

1 Carrefour _____ (operate) since 1959.

2 It _____ (already, open) supermarkets in Brazil and Spain by the time it _____ (diversify) into insurance services.

3 The company _____ (have) supermarkets in Taiwan since 1989.

4 During the 1990s it _____ (expand rapidly) into China and by 2010 it _____ (open) 159 hypermarkets there.

5 Before it _____ (merge) with Promodes in 1999, it _____ (already, take over) Euromarche and Montlaur.

6 The company _____ (run) its online service, ooshop, since 2000.

7 By 2008 year-end, Carrefour _____ (reduce) its overall energy consumption by 13.6% and hypermarkets in France, Italy and Belgium _____ (already, decrease) their energy consumption by 20%.

3 Complete the dialogue using the correct tense (past simple or present perfect) of the verb in brackets.

A: Hi, how's it going? I **1** _____ (not see) you for ages!

B: Oh, fine. I **2** _____ (be) busy with work, you know.

A: Yeah, I know. I **3** _____ (see) Steve yesterday and he **4** _____ (say) you **5** _____ (go) on a leadership course last week.

B: Yes, that's right – we **6** _____ (spend) three days at an outdoor training centre in the middle of nowhere!

A: Sounds fun – we **7** _____ (not have) any training since the computer skills course we **8** _____ (go) on last year, and that **9** _____ (not be) exactly thrilling!

B: Well, I **10** _____ (just hear) there's another leadership course next week – why don't you apply for it?

4 Read the biography of Hong Kong businessman and billionaire, Li Ka Shing. Correct the underlined verbs which are in the wrong tense.

Li Ka Shing's father has died **1** _____ when he has been **2** _____ just 12 years old, leaving him as head of the family. So, he was leaving **3** _____ school to work in a plastics factory to provide for his family, where he has often worked **4** _____ 16-hour days.

His hard work had paid **5** _____ off and he was going **6** _____ on to start his own plastics manufacturing company called Cheung Kong Industries. The company was growing **7** _____ rapidly, and was listed on the Hong Kong Stock Exchange in 1972. Cheung Kong (Holdings) Limited had continued **8** _____ to grow up to the present day, through acquiring major companies such as Hongkong Electric Holdings Limited.

Li Ka Shing move **9** _____ into many other areas since he was starting **10** _____ in business, including telecommunications, shipping, financial services and real estate. Forbes business magazine had estimated **11** _____ the wealth of Li Ka Shing to be 13 billion US dollars in 2005.

Skills

Review! ⊙

2–4 Listen to tracks 2–4, which are from the Student's Book. Notice how the speakers use small talk to 'chat' and how they create an informal atmosphere through their tone and the use of ellipsis.

Making your feelings understood

1 **5** Listen to a speaker say *The meeting was interesting* four times, all with different meanings. Match the recording with the emotions below.

a the speaker is worried _____ **c** the speaker is bored _____

b the speaker is amused _____ **d** the speaker is relieved _____

Listen again and practise saying *The meeting was interesting* using the emotions above.

2 **6** Listen to the sentences below. Match each sentence to the speaker's emotion.

1 The new product is going to be great.	**a** the speaker is worried
2 They haven't followed the brief.	**b** the speaker is amused
3 I think he's on the way.	**c** the speaker is bored
4 The meeting has been cancelled.	**d** the speaker is angry
5 We haven't received our copy of the contract.	**e** the speaker is relieved

3 **7** Look at the following mini-dialogues and <u>underline</u> the stressed words in B's answers.

1 A: Who was at the meeting?
B: Well, Arben was there, but Nora wasn't.
2 A: How was the course?
B: Well, the course was interesting, but the venue was terrible.
3 A: What did you think of the new restaurant?
B: The food was good, but there wasn't much choice.
4 A: What was Paris like?
B: We really enjoyed all the sightseeing, but the weather was awful!

Now listen and check your answers.

Sounding friendly in informal situations ⊙

1 Look at the examples from the recording of the pre-meeting small talk in Unit 1.3, listening 1.05. The speakers are talking about a meal in a restaurant. What are the missing words?

1 A good meal out in Aachen? _____

2 Downstairs or upstairs? _____

3 Good? _____

4 And great food? _____

2 Look at the following informal conversation between colleagues and write down what the full version should be.

A: Meeting OK? **1** _____

B: Really frustrating, actually. **2** _____

A: Oh?

B: Were there 2 hours, didn't decide much. **3** _____

A: Coffee? **4** _____

B: No time – got another meeting! **5** _____

A: Oh no, maybe later? **6** _____

8 Now listen and check your answers.

3 Read the conversation between a customer and supplier. Make these responses shorter and friendlier by taking words out.

A: Would you like a drink before we start? **1** _____

B: Oh, yes please. I'll have a coffee. **2** _____

A: So, how was your journey? **3** _____

B: OK, but the flight was delayed for 45 minutes. **4** _____

A: Was there much traffic on the way here? **5** _____

B: No, it was pretty quiet, actually. **6** _____

CEF Can Do statements

Now you have completed the exercises in this unit, read the following statements. Tick the boxes that apply to you.

	Yes, I can do this.	I think I need more practice.
1 I can use key terms to talk about competitive markets.	☐	☐
2 I can use a range of past tenses to talk about past events.	☐	☐
3 I can use intonation to sound friendly and build business relationships.	☐	☐

If you need more practice on points 1–3, check your Student's Book:

1 Lesson 1.1   **2** Lesson 1.2   **3** Lesson 1.3

Make a note of the areas you want to practise more and how you can do this.

2 Future uncertainty

Vocabulary and Grammar

STEEP analysis

1 What do the abbreviations STEEP and FMCG stand for?

S _____   F _____
T _____   M _____
E _____   C _____
E _____   G _____
P _____

2 Use the clues to find the words.

1 to buy   p_____ (8 letters)

2 very large   m_____ (7 letters)

3 influence   s_____ (5 letters)

4 on the other hand   c_____ (10 letters)

5 natural foods grown with no chemicals

   o_____ (7 letters)

6 food produced from seeds engineered in a laboratory

   g_____ m_____ (11 letters, 8 letters)

7 insufficient supplies   s_____ (9 letters)

8 thinking again   r_____ (13 letters)

3 Complete the text with the words from exercise 2.

In the future, we're going to have to think more carefully about our food supply: food **1** _____ , which have in the past been more common in developing countries, will also start to happen in developed countries. Some scientists have argued that **2** _____ food is the answer: producing crops which are disease and pest-resistant. **3** _____ , environmentalists have argued that **4** _____ food is the way forward. Either way, as consumers become more aware of these arguments, they are **5** _____ the type of food they buy and this will also **6** _____ the market and the products which are available in the future. Food and food processing is a **7**_____ business and the decisions we make about what to **8** _____ as individual consumers will have far-reaching effects.

Consumer goods sectors

1 Complete the expressions for the different types of consumer goods sectors.

1 food and d_____

2 consumer e_____

3 home c_____

4 supermarket r_____

5 health and b_____

6 home e_____

2 Complete the sentences with the expressions from exercise 1.

1 The company specialises in _____ products, such as cosmetics, hair care products, medicines etc.

2 The _____ sector has seen a huge rise over the past few years as more and more people join the rush to get the latest computer technology.

3 Our range of _____ products has everything you need from kitchen and bathroom cleaning to garden maintenance.

4 Sales in Northern Ireland's _____ processing sector grew to £3.2 billion last year, according to the Department of Agriculture and Rural Development.

5 You can now buy all your _____ from our online store, including laptops, TVs, mobiles, PCs and more.

6 _____ giants, such as WalMart and Tesco, are being blamed for the decline in small, independent grocery stores.

Future certainty and uncertainty

1 **Look at the predictions about trends in the consumer goods industry and <u>underline</u> the verbs that are used to talk about the future.**

1 Technology will continue to evolve and impact on consumer habits and expectations.
2 Some people could become fed up with the amount of technology and move back to more face-to-face business.
3 Car manufacturers might consider selling direct to the consumer via their own websites.
4 CO_2 issues in the future may mean that computer manufacturers need to focus more on recycling component parts.
5 Marketing and selling online will probably grow much further, particularly in certain fields of business like retail.
6 Falling birth rates will definitely result in decreased demand and greater competition as the number of consumers fall.
7 Due to increasing health awareness in developed countries, it is highly unlikely that the demand for GM foods will rise.
8 The regulations for companies producing healthcare products are going to become stricter.
9 I guess there may be more global products like Coca-Cola, which is drunk all over the world.
10 It looks probable that the subject of CO_2 emissions will be the dominating subject over the next few years.

Match the sentences above with the correct degree of certainty a–c.

a possible _____

b probable _____

c certain _____

2 **Complete the sentences with the correct expression, depending on how certain the speakers are. Some letters have been given to help you.**

1 I s_____ we'll have to wait until the boss is back from holiday before making that decision. (possible)

2 We m_____ consider the needs of the growing numbers of elderly consumers. (certain)

3 We've been told they _____ definitely move production to the Far East. (certain)

4 It's _____ _____ that the project will go ahead if they don't get any more funding from the government. (probable)

5 It _____ probable that regulations controlling CO_2 emissions will get tougher. (probable)

6 I g_____ we could wait until next week to see if the results of the survey have come back. (possible)

3 **Look at the following pairs of predictions and decide which in each pair is the most certain.**

1 A: I guess we will have to do things differently in the future.
   B: It'll probably be another year before they have broadband in rural areas.
2 A: We might well recruit forty new people in the New Year.
   B: I suppose we'll have to refund them if we don't get the order to them on time.
3 A: It looks probable that the company will offer him a promotion.
   B: There could be a problem with that.
4 A: We may have to move people to other departments.
   B: I'll be back by then.
5 A: It's highly unlikely that the flight will be cancelled because of fog.
   B: Sales could increase over the holiday period.
6 A: Some renewable fuels may even be doing more harm to the environment than oil and gas.
   B: Companies will need to take a more multicultural approach to business.

Skills

Review! 🔘

9–10 Listen to tracks 9–10, which are from the Student's Book. Notice how the speaker organises her presentation the style and discourse markers she uses to link segments of her presentation.

Discourse markers

1 Look at the following examples and <u>underline</u> the discourse markers.

1 So why do we really want to upgrade besides the impact of not doing it?
2 Well, we want to reduce the risk of maintaining …
3 And as you can imagine, as time goes by, that figure's going to go up.
4 Right, I think we should start.
5 So what is our basic approach going to be in Japan?
6 It's important that we upgrade the system … obviously we've been looking into alternatives.

2 Complete the informal presentation with the correct discourse markers. The first letters have been given to help you.

1 S_____ , I'd like to start today by looking at the background to the project. 2 T_____ we'll move on to the current situation and finally we'll discuss where we go from here.
3 O_____ , we've only got an hour, so we'll have to keep it brief. 4 W_____ , let's start with the background … The main point is we might not even get the contract, I
5 m_____ nothing is guaranteed … On the
6 o_____ h_____ , if we do, then we'll have to work quickly to meet the deadlines … And finally, before I hand over, I'd
7 j_____ like to say thanks to everyone for all your hard work so far.

3 Look at the following extracts from a presentation and put them in the right order.

1 I mean, if we stick with the same type of products we've always had, I think we're going to get left behind, so although there is a risk changing the product, I think it's necessary …
2 Right – this is our proposed change – the new product. We wanted to have something new and fresh to present to the market this spring and we think it's time to change our image.
3 So, what do we do now? Well, we've already done some market research which suggests …
4 OK, let's get started.
5 So, as you probably know, this product has been in the pipeline for some time now, and I'd like to give you some information on it …

11 Now listen and check your answers.

CEF Can Do statements

Now you have completed the exercises in this unit, read the following statements. Tick the boxes that apply to you.

	Yes, I can do this.	I think I need more practice.
1 I can use vocabulary connected with a STEEP analysis and the consumer goods sector.	☐	☐
2 I can talk about certain and uncertain future events using a range of structures.	☐	☐
3 I can use discourse markers to help organise an argument and make it easy to follow.	☐	☐

If you need more practice on points 1–3, check your Student's Book:

1 Lesson 2.1/2.2   2 Lesson 2.1   3 Lesson 2.3

Make a note of the areas you want to practise more and how you can do this.

Reading 1
Food Retail in India

Growth, Growth and More Growth

1 _____

Retail is being hailed as India's industry of the future, incited by the country's huge urban middle class population. Food and grocery is the second-largest segment of the retail industry and the potential for new entrants in this segment is enormous, particularly in untapped markets like rural and semi-rural areas. Growing at the rate of 30%, Indian food retail is going to be the major driving force for the retail industry.

2 _____

Fuelled by large disposable incomes, the retail sector is witnessing a remarkable change in consumption patterns, especially in terms of food. Food retailing has come of age – from a period when food items were sold in small road side grocer shops and bazaars by vendors to a stage when food products (processed and groceries) are retailed through supermarket stores where consumers can inspect, select and pick up the products they like in a comfortable ambience and still pay a fair price. Shopping for groceries is no longer a strenuous and uncomfortable affair.

3 _____

The first visible sign of the change in food retailing was seen in the mid-eighties. Around that time a few new food stores were set up in all metro cities in India.

Until the late 1990s, food retailing in the form of hypermarkets, supermarkets and neighbourhood stores was concentrated in the south of the country. The reason being that most entrepreneurs who started organised retail came from southern India and the cost of real estate in the southern region was less than other regions. Since then, however, organised food retailing has emerged across the country, inspired by the presence of high potential markets in the north, west and east as well as the success of some non-food retailers and food services companies in these regions.

4 _____

There are various factors paving the way to revolutionising food retailing in India. Among them are:
- Changing lifestyles and tastes
- Growing need for convenience
- Increasing disposable income
- Increasing numbers of working women
- Change in consumption patterns
- Higher aspirations among youth
- Impact of western lifestyle
- Plastic Revolution – increased use of credit cards and debit cards

With changing food consumption patterns, consumers' need for convenience, choice and value for money, the set-up of the retail format is changing. Indian consumers have always visited about eight to ten outlets to purchase various food products. These outlets include neighbourhood kirana stores, bakeries, fruit and vegetable outlets, dairy booths and chakkies (small flour mills), which is a very time-consuming and unproductive way of shopping for food.

With changing lifestyles, there is a scarcity of time. So, convenience in food shopping is emerging as an important driver of growth for one-stop retail formats that can offer the consumer 'value for time' in addition to 'value for money'. In every retail format, the food trade is growing. A huge increase is expected from the corporate players, which will help grow the entire food retail sector. Retailers are offering a package of convenience and freshness, and have an edge over manufacturers that focus mainly on packaged conveniences.

5 _____

The past 4–5 years have seen increasing activity in food retailing. Various business houses have already planned for investments in the coming 2–3 years. Though the retailers will have to face increasingly demanding customers and intensely competitive rivals, more investments will keep flowing in and the share of the organised food sector will grow rapidly.

Organised food retailing in India is surely poised for a take-off and will provide many opportunities both to existing players as well as new entrants.

Source: *Chillibreeze Solutions PVt Ltd, by Pooja Srivastava*

1 Read the article about food retailing in India and decide which section the following headings refer to.

a The future of food retail
b The food retail story
c Food retail: industry of the future
d Food retail: a changing market
e Drivers for development

2 Read the article again. Are the statements true (T), false (F) or not stated (NS)?

1 Food is the largest sector of the retail industry. _____

2 People don't shop in roadside shops anymore. _____

3 Food retail expanded throughout the country in the 1990s. _____

4 Property in the south of India was cheaper than other regions. _____

5 Changes in the way people live their lives are affecting the food retail industry. _____

6 People have less time and more money and this has changed their shopping habits. _____

7 Big companies are expected to make a small investment in this market in the near future. _____

3 Find words or phrases in the article with the following meanings.

1 encouraged by (paragraph 1) _____

2 unexploited (paragraph 1) _____

3 made larger and stronger (paragraph 2) _____

4 become mature (paragraph 2) _____

5 difficult, demanding (paragraph 2) _____

6 making it easier, helping along (paragraph 5) _____

7 lack (noun) (paragraph 6) _____

8 have an advantage (paragraph 6) _____

9 competitors (paragraph 7) _____

10 ready, prepared (paragraph 8) _____

4 Complete the sentences with the words and phrases from exercise 3. You may need to change the form of the verbs.

1 The new model will mean the company _____ their competitors in this field.

2 The company is _____ for its next phase of expansion, which could include takeovers and mergers.

3 Scientists hope that the data will _____ for a more detailed exploration of Mars.

4 The team have now won twice as many titles as any of their _____ .

5 The resources in the west of the country remain largely _____ due to a lack of infrastructure.

6 _____ the fantastic advertising campaign and the following problems supplying stock, consumers were panic-buying the product, which resulted in a lack of stock.

7 After years of undeveloped potential, are business networking sites finally _____ ?

8 Climate change has led to a _____ of water in many regions.

9 Although demand for the new products has increased, _____ consumer optimism, analysts warn it may not last.

10 After a(n) _____ practice session, the team announced that they were ready for the new season.

Writing 1
Preparing presentation slides

Trends in food shopping

1 Look at the slide from a presentation about Trends in Food Shopping and match the headings to the pictures.

a 'Demand for organic food' _____

b 'Rise of internet retailing' _____

c 'Demand for local produce' _____

d 'Convenience shopping' _____

2 Look at the following sentences from a report about trends in the food retail business in India. Summarise them into bullet points for a presentation slide. Some words have been given to help you.

a Major spending on food and increasing food consumption outside the home represent a significant opportunity for food retailers and food service companies.

Example: Food spending and consumption increasing – opportunity for retailers and service companies.

b Food is the largest share of consumer spending: food products account for about 50 percent of the value of private consumption.

50 percent _____ _____

_____ food.

c Consumers have a growing need for convenience, with less time available for shopping.

Less _____ _____ – _____

_____ needed.

d People spend up to 60 percent of their food bill on unbranded products and this is increasing.

Unbranded _____ _____ _____

_____ _____ _____ _____

increasing.

e Organised food retail presents a unique investment opportunity for corporates looking to diversify.

Food _____ – _____ _____

_____ _____ diversify.

f Food retail is set to attract foreign investment as well as local and national players.

Food _____ _____ _____

_____ _____ _____ investment.

3 Change the bullet points you have written in exercise 2 to high-impact micro-bullet points (three words or less).

a   Food spending increasing _____

b _____

c _____

d _____

e _____

f _____

4 Complete the gaps in the sentences to expand these bullet points, using the correct form of the verbs.

Example: Change in consumption patterns –> Consumption patterns *are changing*.

a Increasing numbers of working women → The numbers of working women _____ _____ .

b Lack of logistics providers → The retail sector _____ _____ logistics providers at present.

c 1990s – development of larger retail stores → In the 1990s larger retail stores _____ .

d Last ten years – more hypermarkets open → In the last ten years, more hypermarkets _____ _____ .

e Next 10 years – global players enter the market? → In the next 10 years, the global players _____ _____ the market.

5 Think about the trends in an area of business or society that you know about or are interested in. (e.g. food retail, electronics, travel, sports). Write five slides to summarise the main points – use both standard bullet and micro-bullet points. Also think about any images you could use.

3 Rewarding performance

Vocabulary and Grammar

Describing earnings

1 Use the clues to find the words which are all synonyms to describe earnings.

1 A fixed amount of money that you earn, usually paid weekly, especially in a job that needs physical skills or strength.
w_____ (4 letters)

2 A generic word to describe the money you receive for doing regular work. p_____ (3 letters)

3 A technical word, often used in advertisements for senior positions and describing money which is included as part of the whole package of working conditions. r_____ (12 letters)

4 The money that a person, region or country earns from work or receives from investments. i_____ (6 letters)

5 Something you are given or money you receive as a result of good performance at work. r_____ (6 letters)

6 Money received by office workers, usually paid directly into employee's bank account every month. s_____ (6 letters)

2 Complete the sentences with the words from exercise 1.

1 The company are offering a very attractive _____ package, including a company car, medical insurance and relocation costs.

2 The basic rate of _____ is relatively low, but it is usually boosted by commission.

3 We have a company suggestions scheme and we give employees a _____ if their suggestion is taken up.

4 The unions are negotiating for an increase in the minimum _____ as workers in this sector have traditionally earned less than elsewhere.

5 Average _____ levels in India have risen in the last few years, creating a bigger middle class who have new demands.

6 The _____ scale for government employees has far more levels than for their private sector counterparts.

Word partnerships with *incentive* and *pay*

1 A business consultant is giving advice about incentive schemes. Choose the best word to complete each gap from the alternatives given below.

'Well, first of all, it's important to **1** _____ an incentive to staff, even if they already have a good pay **2** _____ . The most effective system is one which will work for all levels in the company, not just one **3** _____ incentivise the high achievers. Traditionally, the employees who are the most **4** _____ incentivise are those with less responsibility. **5** _____ incentives, such as **6** _____ pay, are very common, but don't always work for these employees. There are other ways to incentivise **7** _____ achieve better results, for example by offering extra holidays. Remember, perks and incentives work best alongside good pay **8** _____ and working conditions. When setting up the scheme, it's important to brief staff fully on how it works: just telling them there is a new incentive **9** _____ may even have the opposite effect of demotivating them. Finally, you need to be sure that incentives are not just about pay **10** _____ , they are about making the staff feel valued and motivating them to perform better.'

	A	**B**	**C**
1	arrange	provide	take
2	rate	package	scheme
3	designed to	arranged for	planned to
4	aware of	responsible to	difficult to
5	Bonus	Financial	Reward
6	high-performance	bonus-related	performance-related
7	staff in	staff to	labour to
8	packages	conditions	terms
9	finance	pay	programme
10	rises	executive	conditions

2 Complete the sentences with *pay* or *payment(s)*.

1 The presenter is set to receive a 25 percent _____ rise for staying on the show.

2 Union representatives are seeking a new _____ offer in negotiations with the company today.

3 The new regulation would ensure borrowers are alerted to the risks of loans with variable _____ .

4 Performance-related _____ deals, whereby executives receive bonus _____ , have been criticised by unions.

5 In some cases, more flexible _____ terms can be arranged.

Compound nouns

1 Match the words to make compound nouns. There is one extra word you don't need to use.

1 operating cash	a rates
2 annual base	b value
3 increased shareholder	c revenue
4 customer retention	d incentives
5 new product	e wages
6 short-term cash	f salary
	g flow

2 Complete the sentences with the expressions from exercise 1.

1 The CEO's package last year included payments of $856,000 in addition to his _____ of $364,000.

2 The true success of the marketing campaign should be measured by including _____ as well as how many new customers it attracted.

3 The company said it has implemented new pay packages, which include deferring _____ into medium-term share options.

4 The company has announced a € 60 million _____ for this quarter, up 20% on last quarter.

5 In a statement, the company said it believed the acquisition of the two new companies would lead to _____ through greater market share.

6 Penetration of new overseas markets for the leading mobile phone companies has led to an increase in _____ .

3 Complete the gaps using the correct form of the word from the box. There is one word you do not need to use.

> compensate   equity-base   increase   operate   stretched   compare

1 By setting _____ goals that are difficult to attain, you risk demotivating the workforce.

2 The positive development of volumes and _____ profit continued for the company's Shanghai subsidiary.

3 The remuneration package is based on responsibilities, experience and compensation levels for similar positions in _____ companies.

4 Our _____ programme for senior executives includes an annual base salary, stock options and bonuses.

5 Many companies were less generous in allocating stock options and other _____ awards last year.

4 Choose two words from the words in brackets which make an appropriate compound noun to complete the sentences.

1 [product / retention / customer / revenue] The majority of the company's _____ is derived from specific one-time installations.

2 [value / profit / shareholder / operating] The company's _____ is expected to be up on last year due to rising demand.

3 [base / flow / salary / cash] The company director, according to sources, plans to increase the sales director's _____ this season to $2 million, instead of the planned $1.5 million.

4 [goals / stretch / incentives / cash] Providing _____ to small companies may encourage them to go green, a report claims.

Review! 👁

12–13 Listen to tracks 12–13, which are from the Student's Book. Notice how the speakers use vague language in their negotiation to show their understanding and also as a bargining technique.

Vague language

1 **14** Listen to the following examples from negotiations and complete the sentences with the missing words. Contractions, like *I've*, count as one word.

1 We _____ _____ _____ _____

_____ _____ performance related.

2 I actually thought that _____ _____

_____ _____ _____ _____

_____ _____ _____ _____

salary.

3 I was also doing the second job _____ _____

_____ _____ _____ _____ .

4 _____ _____ _____ _____

3 weeks.

Now sort the sentences into two groups.

a Collaborative strategy: _____

b Competitive strategy: _____

Finally, listen to the sentences again and try to match the model.

2 Look at the following statements and try to make the underlined sections vaguer. You may also need to add in some words or phrases.

1 I want to get a promotion in the next two years.
2 We'll work on that idea in the future.
3 I'm not happy with the salary, the working conditions, the atmosphere …
4 I've had a big increase in my responsibilities – looking after new clients, managing more staff …
5 We will make some changes to the department next quarter.

3a **15** Listen to the following short dialogues and complete the phrases for clarification.

1 A: I've sort of got behind with the schedule, so, you know …

B: So _____ _____ _____

_____ you need more time to finish the project?

2 A: I think we need to look at working conditions and all that kind of thing.

B: _____ 'that kind of thing' _____

_____ _____ salary and holidays?

3 A: It'll probably be ready in about 3 weeks.

B: _____ _____ sure?

4 A: We might not get an answer straight away.

B: _____ _____ _____ we'll have to wait?

b In general, we stress the key words we want to check, and our voice goes up at the end of a question.

Listen to the dialogues again. <u>Underline</u> the stressed words and mark the intonation with an arrow ↑ or ↓.

c Now listen again and try to match the model.

4 A's statements use vague language, so B asks questions to clarify. Put B's clarification questions in the right order.

1 A: I'd have to check with head office before we went ahead.
B: it's definite so mean not you?
2 A: I think it's somewhere in the region of $40,000.
B: are that you sure how of?
3 A: The project has been held up by a number of factors which were beyond our control.
B: saying you're is what so schedule it's behind?
4 A: We haven't been told the exact date yet.
B: date know mean we so don't the you?

CEF Can Do statements

Now you have completed the exercises in this unit, read the following statements. Tick the boxes that apply to you.

	Yes, I can do this.	I think I need more practice.
1 I can use key vocabulary to discuss pay and performance.	☐	☐
2 I understand how to form compound nouns.	☐	☐
3 I can use vague language to negotiate more effectively.	☐	☐

If you need more practice on points 1–3, check your Student's Book:

1 Lesson 3.1   **2** Lesson 3.2   **3** Lesson 3.3

Make a note of the areas you want to practise more and how you can do this.

4 Fostering creativity

Vocabulary and Grammar

Word formations connected with creativity

1 Look at the extract from a talk by a consultant to a group of managers about how to improve performance in their company and complete the gaps with the correct word.

'You may think the R&D Department is the place for exciting and interesting new **1** _____ or that thinking of new and original ideas, ie **2** _____, is just something people in the design or marketing departments need, but in fact, it's important to encourage this in every area of the company. Getting staff to use their **3** _____ to come up with solutions to problems they encounter in their daily work can be very productive. In addition, this can help to encourage **4** _____ between staff: working together to solve a problem can improve overall communication and team-building. It's not always easy, of course: getting agreement or **5** _____ of beliefs may take time. In cases where there is a wide **6** _____ of opinion and a decision is proving difficult, it may be worth exploring the issue in more depth. Thinking of new ideas and solutions is just the beginning, the next step is **7** _____ – putting the ideas into practice. People often resist new ideas or **8** _____ because they don't like change, but if they have been involved in their development, they are more likely to support them. So, the key is to get people involved in the creative and problem-solving process right from the start.'

2 Complete the sentences by writing the correct form of the word given brackets at the end of the sentence.

1 Although difficult to work with, he is recognised as a key _____ in the company, and he brings in many new ideas. (innovate)

2 The company is rolling out its _____ of SAP across its global operations after a successful pilot scheme in the Czech Republic. (implement)

3 _____ industries, like music, TV and film, should look at forming deeper relationships with mobile applications developers. (create)

4 Although the participants had _____ opinions, the various opinions and views produced a very interesting discussion. (diverge)

5 The government is keen to bring about greater _____ with other European countries. (converge)

6 The museum has unveiled a new _____ exhibit which will guide visitors through the history of the castle. (interact)

7 Many famous _____, such as Biro, Dunlop and Diesel, gave their names to the products they invented. (invent)

8 I'm afraid the new product is rather _____ – there are very few changes from the old one. (imagine)

3 One word is wrong in each of the sentences below. <u>Underline</u> the mistake and write the correct word at the end of the sentence.

1 Their products are always very imaginary, with lots of unusual features. _____

2 It's important that we get a converging of opinions by the end of the meeting. _____

3 We'll need to think of new and inventionary ways to solve these problems. _____

4 The data confirmed the growth divergement within the different countries in the Eurozone. _____

5 The new feature of the game is real-time interactiveness. _____

6 This is good news for the region, with the creativeness of at least 1,000 new jobs. _____

7 Intriguing, useful and surprising, the PC Road Show will bring together some of the most innovating computer products of the year. _____

8 The implementory of the new strategy will probably take at least a year from start to finish. _____

Past modals

1 Match the past modals in sentences 1–6 with their use a–e.

1 If only we'd taken the other route, we could've been there by now.
2 They should've realised they needed an export licence – they've exported there before.
3 We've sold far more than last year, so our turnover must have increased.
4 We shouldn't have spent so much on advertising, now there's nothing left for promotional samples.
5 He might have sent a reply, I haven't checked my emails yet.
6 Sari looks really depressed – she can't have got the job.

a Something that was advisable in the past. *(two answers)*
b The speaker is sure that this is the result of something that happened.
c It's impossible that this happened.
d A past possibility, which did not come true.
e It's possible that this happened, but the speaker is not completely sure.

2 Match the two halves of the sentences.

1 They are really late for the meeting –	a they can't have spellchecked it.
2 He's not in the office today –	b we could have sent it by air.
3 We're going to miss the deadline –	c it must have been delivered to the wrong address.
4 There are too many mistakes in the letter –	d there must have been a traffic jam.
5 I'll see if I can find the samples, but	e we shouldn't have spent so long discussing the prototype.
6 We haven't received the order –	f we should have agreed to lower the prices.
7 If we'd known they wanted immediate delivery	g he might have taken a day off.
8 Now we're going to lose the contract –	h they might have been left at the conference.

3 Complete the sentences using the correct form of the verb in brackets.

1 We haven't got enough stock, we _____ (order) more last week.
2 They're taking a long time – I suppose they _____ (have to) stop for petrol or perhaps the traffic is bad.
3 If I'd known there were going to be so many people, I _____ (book) a bigger meeting room.
4 All the directors are driving brand-new cars – the company _____ (have) a good year!
5 It's going to take ages for the system to restart, I _____ (shut) it down.
6 I wonder why he's arrived so early – he _____ (see) the email about the later starting time, because it was sent out yesterday and he had a day off.
7 They've had the whole office redecorated and bought new furniture – it _____ (cost) a fortune!
8 The new system is much faster and easier to manage – we _____ (change) over years ago!

Skills

16–17 Listen to tracks 16–17, which are from the Student's Book. Notice how the speakers use evaluative metaphors and idioms to evaluate ideas positively and negatively, in this part of the decision-making process.

Evaluative metaphors and idioms 🅞

1 Complete the metaphor or idiom with the correct word from the box.

with	on	around	into	balance	down

1 It's _____ to you to make that decision.

2 I'm sure we can find a way _____ the problem.

3 We tried to get a _____ between what younger consumers wanted and what older consumers liked about the product.

4 If we pay for the added cover, it's a serious cost _____ top.

5 I have an issue _____ the delivery time – it's too long.

6 Having a lot of extra meetings eats _____ the time we have available to actually do the work.

All these metaphors and idioms can be used in the decision-making process. Which of them are used to evaluate positively and which are used to evaluate negatively?

Positive: _____   Negative: _____

Not positive or negative: _____

2 **18** Listen to an extract from a meeting. Hitesh, Iona and Dave are discussing their department's budget for the next year.

1 Does Iona agree with the budget?
2 What does Dave suggest?
3 What is Iona's action point from this part of the meeting?

3 Listen again and complete the sentences.

1 Iona: … I think the budget we've been given is _____

   _____ …

2 Iona: … don't say you're going to cut that – it'd be _____

   _____ !

3 Dave: … because we've already got _____

   _____ for replacing …

4 Iona: Yeah, actually, that's _____ _____

   _____ _____ .

5 Iona: … what we're paying now in maintenance costs is

   _____ .

6 Hitesh: _____ _____ _____

   _____ , Iona …

Which of the expressions from the meeting are used positively or negatively?

Positive: _____   Negative: _____

4 Use some of the metaphors and idioms from exercises 1 and 3 to respond to these situations in the decision-making process.

1 A: Well, we could always cut back on overtime.
   B: *(positive) Yes, _____ . Let's look into that.*

2 A: The suppliers want to double the prices.
   B: *(negative) That's _____ ! How can they justify that?*

3 A: Would you like me to contact the clients and discuss it?
   B: *(positive) I'd _____ . Thanks.*

4 A: The quality is great, but the suppliers just don't seem flexible on delivery times.
   B: *(positive) Don't worry. I'm sure we'll find _____ .*

5 A: Do you think we could contact the client and ask for an extension?
   B: *(negative) I really _____ going back to the client and asking for more time.*

19 Now listen to the model and compare your answers. Finally, listen again and try to match the model.

CEF Can Do statements

Now you have completed the exercises in this unit, read the following statements. Tick the boxes that apply to you.

	Yes, I can do this.	I think I need more practice.
1 I can use appropriate word forms to talk about creativity.	☐	☐
2 I can use modals to criticise past actions and explore alternative solutions.	☐	☐
3 I can use metaphors and idioms to evaluate decisions.	☐	☐

If you need more practice on points 1–3, check your Student's Book:

1 Lesson 4.1   **2** Lesson 4.2   **3** Lesson 4.3

Make a note of the areas you want to practise more and how you can do this.

Reading 2
Entrepreneurship: two schools of thought

Entrepreneurs: born or made?

Are entrepreneurs born or made? The question is not asked out of idle curiosity. It goes to the heart of how we should encourage budding entrepreneurs.

It affects how – and indeed whether – organisations should spend their resources teaching and advising people about entrepreneurship.

Entrepreneurs are Made

Doug Richard is the founder of School for Startups and was a panellist on the television show Dragon's Den*. He said: 'There is no doubt that there is an aptitude involved and some people have more of it and some people have less, just as some people will be adequate entrepreneurs and some will be extraordinary ones. But all people who are successful need huge amounts of training and support and learning along the way, so by definition, entrepreneurs are made.'

He added: 'I could take almost anyone and with time or training make him or her an adequate entrepreneur. And I could take someone with aptitude and make him or her a great one. The vital ingredient is the training and not the aptitude.'

Lara Morgan is another who believes that entrepreneurs are made rather than born that way. She founded Pacific Direct, a business that provides toiletries to hotels, and sold it in 2008 for £20m. She has started a new business called *Functionally*, which aims to inspire growth firms.

'Your circumstances dictate whether you become an entrepreneur or not,' said Morgan. 'My dad had set up his own company but it was not successful. He went bankrupt and I was really determined not to make the mistakes he made. A lot of it is about wanting a better life for your children. I never wanted to be the only parent in the class who could not afford to let their children go on the school trip, which happened to me when I was young. It is about having a determination to succeed and that is not something you are born with.'

They are Born That Way

Tim Roupell belongs to the school which believes entrepreneurs are born. He founded *Daily Bread*, a sandwich firm, which he sold in 2008. 'Entrepreneurs are born because you need to have a slightly rebellious streak in you to be an entrepreneur,' said Roupell. 'You are someone who likes being in control of your own destiny rather than just joining a company and climbing your way up the corporate ladder.'

He added: 'You can teach the basics of entrepreneurship. But you can't teach someone that they are going to have to take all the responsibility themselves and that they are going to have to provide all the drive themselves to achieve their goals.

'There is a danger in encouraging people to become entrepreneurs because not everybody is suited to it and it would be absolutely wrong to encourage the wrong people to do it. You mustn't set people up to fail.'

Claire Young is another person who thinks along the same lines. She is a former finalist of the television show, *The Apprentice*. She is in the process of launching two new businesses – a social enterprise for girls called Girls Out Loud and a speaking agency for schools.

'I work with young people in schools across the country, teaching them about enterprise,' said Young. 'You can teach people about enterprise and culturally embed it in their minds, but if they haven't been born with the drive and the tenacity and the passion, it isn't going to happen ...

'Success is down to the hunger and passion that you are born with. If you have it, you can't switch it off. It doesn't matter when you are born or who you are born to. Entrepreneurs come in all shapes and sizes.'

Source: *The Sunday Times 4th July 2010, by Rachel Bridge*

*First launched in Japan, *Dragon's Den* is a TV programme, which is now an international brand, with TV versions in different countries around the world. Entrepreneurs pitch for investment in the Den from the 5 'Dragons'. The 'Dragons' are venture capitalists willing to invest their own money in exchange for equity.

1 Read the article and decide which of the following is the best summary.

1 The article concludes that entrepreneurs are born, not made.

_____

2 There are strong arguments on both sides about whether entrepreneurs are born or made but the article does not reach any conclusions. _____

3 The article concludes that entrepreneurs are made, not born.

_____

2 Read the article again. Are the statements true (T), false (F) or not stated (NS)?

1 The writer of the article thinks it's not important whether entrepreneurs are born or made. _____

2 Doug Richard says that it takes a lot of money to train successful entrepreneurs. _____

3 Lara Morgan's father had his own business. _____

4 Lara Morgan became motivated to succeed because of her father's failed business. _____

5 Tim Roupell says entrepreneurs want to join a company and get promoted. _____

6 Tim Roupell thinks it's a good idea to encourage everyone to become entrepreneurs. _____

7 Claire Young has already set up two companies. _____

8 Claire Young believes if you have a desire for success you can't switch it off. _____

3 Find expressions in the article with the following meanings:

1 an interest in something with no particular purpose

_____

2 showing signs of potential _____

3 to start a new company _____

4 wanting to defy authority for no particular reason _____

5 has the same opinion _____

6 to make something an integral part of _____

4 Match the expressions from the text with the correct meaning.

1 aptitude (paragraph 3)	a determination to continue
2 vital (paragraph 4)	b determine, influence
3 dictate (paragraph 6)	c a natural ability or skill
4 drive (paragraph 8)	d is based on
5 is suited to (paragraph 9)	e motivation
6 set someone up (paragraph 9)	f essential
7 tenacity (paragraph 11)	g is right for someone
8 is down to (paragraph 12)	h give someone the opportunity

5 Complete the sentences with the correct expressions from exercises 3 and 4. You may need to change the form of the word.

1 If you want to succeed, you need to show a lot of _____ ; it's _____ that you don't give up!

2 A job like sales _____ someone like you – you have a lot of _____ and you can take the initiative.

3 Fortunately, the meeting went very smoothly and there were no real disagreements as we were all _____ .

4 He has a real _____ for sport and is great with people. He would make an excellent leisure centre manager.

5 The prize for the competition, which is designed to encourage _____ authors, is a publishing deal worth $10,000.

6 Our sales results for the year will _____ whether we get a pay rise or not.

Writing 2
Describing a process

1 Look at this description of a recruitment process and complete the gaps with the correct form of the verb from the box.

write   must return   will request   promote   send   appoint
can provide   hold   arrange   need   invite   update

A vacancy arises. Sometimes this is due to the creation of a new job, on other occasions it may be because an existing member of staff **1** _____ or is retiring.

The job description **2** _____ and an employment specification **3** _____ . The job description lists the duties of the job while the specification gives details of the experience, skills which **4** _____ to carry out the job.

Application forms **5** _____ out along with copies of the job description and employee specification. These **6** _____ on or before the closing date that has been set.

A shortlist* is compiled of applicants who are going to **7** _____ to attend an interview.

Interviews **8** _____ . Feedback **9** _____ upon request.

References **10** _____ . The successful candidate **11** _____ , and training **12** _____ .

* list of candidates who have been selected from a larger group of applicants

2 Look at the following description of a project management process. Choose the best word for each gap from the choices below.

The **1** _____ stage is to agree a precise specification for the project, known as 'Terms of Reference'. Project terms of reference also provide an essential discipline and framework to keep the project on track.

This is **2** _____ the planning stage, when the project is **3** _____ into its key components: time, team, activities, resources and financials. Complex projects will have a number of activities running in parallel. Some parts of the project will need other parts of the project to be completed before they can begin or progress.

The next **4** _____ is communication: explain the project plan to your project team – and to any other interested people and groups. Generally try to establish your team as soon as possible.

5 _____ you need to agree and delegate project actions. Make sure activities are very clearly described and explained to those responsible for a task.

6 _____ the project you need to manage and motivate as well as measure and review project progress. Poor communication at this stage can **7** _____ lost time and misunderstandings amongst the team.

8 _____ the project is complete, it is essential to review and report on performance **9** _____ the project team know how they have done.

10 _____ , follow up the project: train, support, measure and report results and benefits.

1 A firstly	**B** beginning	**C** initial
2 A leading to	**B** followed by	**C** preceded by
3 A separating	**B** broken down	**C** broken up
4 A stage	**B** platform	**C** process
5 A After this	**B** Lately	**C** Latterly
6 A While	**B** At the same time	**C** During
7 A lead to	**B** be caused by	**C** result
8 A Finally	**B** Once	**C** Then
9 A as	**B** because	**C** so
10 A At last	**B** In summary	**C** Finally

3 Look at the following diagram of the development of a business process. This process could be adapted for many different business areas (e.g. Accounting and Finance, Sales and Telemarketing, or Web Design and Development)

Business Process Development
- Analyse
  - Create Model
    - Instigate
      - Monitor
        - Improve Model
          - Automate & Finalise
            - Implement

Write a short description of the process, using appropriate verb forms and linking structures (about a 100 words).

5 Organisational cultures

Vocabulary and Grammar

Vocabulary to talk about organisations

1 Match words 1–7 with words a–g to make expressions to talk about organisations. You need to use one word twice and another word is not used.

1 reward	**a** at work
2 dress	**b** culture
3 expense	**c** structure
4 task	**d** systems
5 atmosphere	**e** accounts
6 organisational	**f** code
7 role	**g** budget

2 Complete the sentences with the expressions from exercise 1.

1 We've had some problems with employees using their _____ for private purposes, so we've had to cut right back.

2 The _____ of my previous company was very hierarchical, whereas here it's much flatter.

3 The bank reviewed its _____ after the financial crisis.

4 Companies with a strong _____ are believed to be very stable, but poor at implementing change.

5 The company operates a strict _____ with client-facing employees expected to wear suits.

6 The company has a very strong _____ and is really team and project orientated.

7 The _____ is one of the main reasons why I love my job: everyone is very positive and we all enjoy working together.

3 Use the clues to find the words to talk about organisational cultures.

1 A set of actions which is the official or accepted way of doing something. p_____ (10 letters)

2 Money available to spend on something. b_____ (6 letters)

3 Ways of doing things or behaviours which are common to a group of people. n_____ (5 letters)

4 Different sections of a company, e.g. R&D, d_____ (11 letters)

5 Instructions that state the way things are or should be done. r_____ (5 letters)

6 Key beliefs for a company or culture. v_____ (6 letters)

7 A person's character, e.g. friendly, relaxed. p_____ (11 letters)

4 Choose the best word to complete each gap from the alternatives given below. Put a circle round the letter, A, B or C, of the word you choose.

There are many different types of 1 _____ structure: hierarchical, centralised, decentralised, and these all affect the decisions a company makes, from strategy to attitude to employees. In a hierarchical company, there will be many layers of management, often with many official 2 _____ for everything from taking holidays to ordering stationery. 3 _____ – what employees are allowed to wear – is often controlled as are status 'symbols' like company cars, personal offices, etc. Even 4 _____ , important for employees who have to entertain clients, can be dependent on your level in the company. Clearly, all of these factors affect the 5 _____ – companies where there are too many regulations and levels of hierarchy can be stressful places to work. However, these regulations can be a strength and they are certainly a key feature of companies with a(n) 6 _____ .

1	**A** organisation	**B** organised	**C** organisational
2	**A** process	**B** procedures	**C** proceeds
3	**A** Dressing code	**B** Dress code	**C** Dress wear
4	**A** expense accounts	**B** expensive accounts	**C** cash accounts
5	**A** atmosphere in work	**B** environment of work	**C** atmosphere at work
6	**A** task culture	**B** organisational culture	**C** role culture

Asking questions effectively

1 Put the words in the correct order to make questions.

1 A: we / short / take / don't / break / a / why / ?

_____

B: Good idea!

2 A: do / to / don't / we / finish / have / by / we / 4 / ?

B: No, I don't think so.

3 A: having / when / launch / we're / party / do / you / know / the / ?

_____

B: Not until next spring.

4 A: up / have / meeting / the / set / would / time / you / to / room / ?

_____

B: I should think so.

5 A: email / didn't / an / why / send / me / you / ?

_____

B: Sorry, our system was down.

6 A: could / was / off / I / take / if / tomorrow / I / wondering / ?

_____

B: Well, it's a bit short notice.

7 A: We've exceeded our targets this quarter.

B: we / have – big / though / lost / contract / even / we / that / ?

_____

2 Match questions 1–7 from exercise 1 with their functions a–g.

a ask somebody to do something _____

b check understanding or seek agreement _____

c show surprise or interest _____

d show politeness _____

e make a suggestion _____

f criticise somebody or show dissatisfaction _____

g ask for information _____

3 Tag questions, such as question 2 in exercise 1 above, are very common in spoken English for checking or seeking agreement. Look at the questions below and complete the tag.

1 He'll have to stay here, _____ _____?

2 We weren't that far away, _____ _____?

3 I'd better go, _____ _____?

4 They'd rather we took the first option, _____ _____?

5 I think we should renew the contract, _____ _____?

6 They said they'd be here by 9, _____ _____?

7 You couldn't print this off for me, _____ _____?

8 Let's take a break now, _____ _____?

4 Complete the following mini-dialogues showing different types of question.

1 A: I can't see the point of looking at this contract.

B: _____ ? *(show surprise or interest)*

2 A: _____ _____ you meet your deadline? *(criticise someone or show dissatisfaction)*

B: I'm sorry, we've had a lot of work over the last 2 weeks.

3 A: What do you think we should do?

B: _____ _____ _____ reconsider the plan to redevelop the park area? *(make a suggestion)*

4 A: I think we should get together soon to discuss this – _____ _____ organise a meeting for tomorrow morning? *(ask someone to do something)*

B: Sure, no problem.

5 A: You've got all the handouts for the meeting, _____ _____? *(check understanding or seek agreement)*

B: Yes, don't worry, they're right here.

6 A: _____ _____ _____ you to help me with this? *(ask somebody to do something / show politeness)*

B: Yes, sure, what can I do?

Skills

Strategically summarising a position

1 Complete the expressions for strategically summarising a discussion or negotiation with the words in the box.

point	honest	mean	about	think	saying	talking
mean	with					

1 I'm just _____ that attitudes need to change.

2 I _____ , to be _____ _____ you, we really need to look at this again.

3 What I _____ is we can't afford to get this wrong.

4 My _____ is we've only got 6 weeks to complete this.

5 What we're _____ _____ is producing another prototype from scratch.

6 So this _____ that we have to change all our prices.

2 🎧 **23** Listen again to the examples from the meeting in 5.3 and fill in the missing words.

1 Doz: Having discussed it with them, _____ _____ _____ ownership, I think.

2 Laura: ... I think they've got to be very customer facing and their attitude has got to change, _____ _____ _____ _____ _____ _____ .

3 Laura: I'm _____ _____ _____ . I think they're fabulous with customers.

4 Laura: What _____ _____ _____ that if the customer doesn't ring them back …

5 Doz: I agree, _____ _____ _____ _____ it's one of those things …

3 Use the expressions from exercises 1 and 2 above to strategically summarise your position.

1 You think the main point is staff morale.

I think _____ _____ _____ staff morale.

2 You don't mean that the team are lazy.

_____ _____ _____ _____ .

I think they work very hard.

3 You have already mentioned that the sales team need to change their attitude.

I think the sales team need to change their attitude, _____ _____ _____ _____ _____ .

4 You agree but you mention that there may be other reasons.

I agree but _____ _____ _____ there may be other reasons.

5 You want to emphasise that no one seems to take responsibility.

_____ _____ _____ *is that no one seems to take responsibility.*

6 The main issue for you is that cost needs to be considered.

_____ _____ _____ *that we have to think about cost.*

🎧 **23** **Now listen to the model and compare your answers. Finally, listen again and try to match the model.**

CEF Can Do statements

Now you have completed the exercises in this unit, read the following statements. Tick the boxes that apply to you.

	Yes, I can do this.	I think I need more practice.
1 I can use appropriate vocabulary to describe organisational cultures.	☐	☐
2 I can use accurate structures to ask questions effectively.	☐	☐
3 I can use strategic summaries to support an argument.	☐	☐

If you need more practice on points 1–3, check your Student's Book:

1 Lesson 5.1   **2** Lesson 5.2   **3** Lesson 5.3

Make a note of the areas you need to practise more and how you can do this.

6 Working across cultures

Vocabulary related to culture

1 Decide which of the alternatives a–g the speaker is talking about. Match the sentences to the correct alternative.

1	The atmosphere is good and we all get on well together.	**a**	face
2	Unfortunately he doesn't have any self-respect anymore.	**b**	sociality rights
3	His birthplace has always given him a strong sense of who he is.	**c**	rapport
4	He wants to convey an image of being tough, but I don't think he is really.	**d**	social inclusion
5	I'm afraid he can't do that job – he doesn't have the right level of skills.	**e**	dignity
6	I think everyone should be entitled to free education, health and dental care.	**f**	competence
7	It's important that all people benefit from the social entitlements of their community.	**g**	identity

Nouns to make positive and negative judgements

1 Use the clues to find the words.

1 An active disagreement between people with opposing opinions or principles. c_____ (8 letters)

2 The combined power of a group of things when they are working together which is greater than the total power achieved by each working separately. s_____ (7 letters)

3 The characteristic of being clear and easy to understand. t_____ (12 letters)

4 A situation, person or thing that needs attention and needs to be dealt with or solved. p_____ (7 letters)

5 An occasion or situation that makes it possible to do something. o_____ (11 letters)

6 An occasion which allows something to be done. c_____ (6 letters)

2 Look at the list of verbs which form collocations with the nouns in exercise 1. Write a noun from exercise 1 next to the correct verb.

Verbs	Nouns	Prepositions
give/stand/create/have/get		
raise/resolve/avoid		
seize/explore/exploit		
create/seek		
inhibit/lack/enhance		
solve/cause/have		

Now look at the prepositions in the box below and write them next to the correct verb + noun collocations.

between/among/with   for/to   to/of   between/of   with   in/between

3 Complete the sentences with the collocations from exercise 2.

1 The key to successful mergers and acquisitions is to _____ your existing businesses.

2 The team must _____ every _____ score in the upcoming match, if they want to win the competition.

3 In order to _____ getting the contract, we need to start working on the bid now.

4 There seemed to be regular communication problems in our company, so weekly meetings were set up in order to _____ the different departments.

5 93% of websites _____ their ad tags, the pieces of code that track the performance of online advertising campaigns, according to a new survey.

6 The new regulations are designed to _____ financial institutions. It's important to make sure that financial procedures are clear and easy to understand.

Reporting verbs

1 **Use the clues to find the key verbs for reporting. The first letter has been given to help you.**

1 To tell someone that you are sorry for having done something.

a_____ (9 letters)

2 To have the same opinion or to accept a suggestion or idea.

a_____ (5 letters)

3 To tell someone that you will certainly do something.

p_____ (7 letters)

4 To say that you will not do or accept something.

r_____ (6 letters)

5 To say that something is not true. d_____ (4 letters)

6 To talk or behave in a way that gives someone confidence to do something. e_____ (9 letters)

7 To express to someone that you are pleased with something they have done. t_____ (5 letters)

8 To ask someone if they would like you to do something.

o_____ (5 letters)

2 **Match sentences 1–8 below with the verbs from exercise 1 to show what each sentence is illustrating.**

1 'I think you should apply for it – you've got all the right skills.'

_____

2 'I'll call you back first thing tomorrow.' _____

3 'That's great. I really appreciate you doing that.' _____

4 'Shall I sort out the address list?' _____

5 'I'm in favour of increasing the targets.' _____

6 'I'm so sorry we're late.' _____

7 'We're not starting the whole project again, it's impossible.'

_____

8 'I never said anything about the salary.' _____

3 **Now use the verbs from exercise 1 to change the sentences in exercise 2 into the reported form.**

1 She _____ him _____ _____ for it.

2 He _____ _____ _____ her back first thing.

3 She _____ her _____ _____ it.

4 He _____ _____ _____ out the address list.

5 He _____ _____ _____ the targets.

6 They _____ _____ _____ late.

7 They _____ _____ _____ the whole project again.

8 She _____ _____ anything about the salary.

4 **Choose the best option from the words in brackets to complete the sentence.**

1 The employees agreed _____ overtime for the month. (the contract to work / to work)

2 The manager refused _____ the money. (refunding / to refund)

3 The CEO thanked the staff _____ support. (for their continuing / to continue)

4 The boss _____ an extra day's holiday. (offered to us / offered to give us)

5 The man was arrested but _____ any money from the company. (denied to take / denied taking)

6 My boss encouraged _____ for promotion. (me to apply / me applying)

7 The company _____ the goods so late. (apologised to send / apologised for sending)

8 They've promised _____ our next order on time. (us to deliver / to deliver)

Skills

Review! 🎯

24–25 Listen to tracks 24–25, which are from the Student's Book. Notice the stages described of building a team and also any metaphors used to describe progress in track 24.

The stages of building a team and using metaphors in business 🎯

1 What are the four stages of team-building?

1 f_____   3 n_____

2 s_____   4 p_____

Match the stages to their definitions below.

a the group usually finds some of the initial guidelines and expectations are unsuitable _____

b the initial stage where the team gets to know each other and makes some provisional guidelines _____

c the group begins to work together, having overcome the main issues in the previous stage _____

d the group performs effectively, and productivity is high _____

2 26 Listen to these extracts from meetings and complete the metaphors.

1 We're going to _____ _____ and do this checking.

2 You could probably have done it every two months and _____ _____ _____ .

3 Did we _____ _____ _____ _____ at Staines by checking it every month?

4 I think that we should _____ _____ from that point …

5 Unfortunately, the business has been _____ _____ since Dan retired.

6 Well, it's good to see things are _____ _____ again now.

7 Sorry, could you go over that again, I'm _____ _____ .

3 Look at the metaphors in exercise 2 and decide which function they perform.

a a desire for progress _____

b a lack of progress _____

c progress _____

4 Respond to the prompts using an appropriate form of a metaphor from exercise 2.

1 You want to change the topic.
   Can we _____ _____ to the next point?

2 You don't know what stage the project is at and you'd like a recap.
   I'm afraid I'm _____ _____ . Could we just recap where we are?

3 You're pleased that the project has been approved by senior management.
   I'm pleased to say we can _____ _____ with the project now.

4 You're concerned that you did too much analysis and lost time.
   I think we _____ _____ _____ _____ on the analysis and lost time.

5 You've made good progress and you want to maintain that.
   Let's try to _____ _____ _____ with this if we can.

6 You want to explain that the project pace has become quicker.
   We're _____ _____ at a rapid rate now.

27 Now listen to the model and compare your answers. Finally, listen again and try to match the model.

CEF Can Do statements

Now you have completed the exercises in this unit, read the following statements. Tick the boxes that apply to you.

	Yes, I can do this.	I think I need more practice.
1 I can use appropriate noun collocations to make positive and negative judgements in written and spoken business communication.	☐	☐
2 I can use direct and indirect reported speech with questions.	☐	☐
3 I can understand the different stages of team-building and can use metaphors to describe progress in business.	☐	☐

If you need more practice on points 1–3, check your Student's Book:

1 Lesson 6.2   2 Lesson 6.1   3 Lesson 6.3

Make a note of the areas you want to practise more and how you can do this.

Reading 3
Geert Hofstede

1 Before you read the article, think about what you know about Geert Hofstede: who is he and why is he famous? Why has his research become so important in business today? Then read the article and check your answers.

Cultural Diversity

1 _____

Geert Hofstede (b 1928) is a Dutch academic who has also spent long periods in industry, most notably at IBM. He has become known for pioneering research on national and organisational cultures. Much of his subsequent thinking was based on a monumental six-year research project in the late 1960s and early 1970s into the working of a giant international corporation, originally known by the pseudonym HERMES and later revealed as IBM. The management of cultural diversity is becoming a significant issue for companies of all sizes, not just multinationals. The rise of global business – leading to an increase in the number of joint ventures and cross-border partnerships, greater co-operation within the European Union and business's need to embrace people from a variety of ethnic backgrounds and cultures, have all contributed to the need to develop cultural sensitivity. Ignorance or insensitivity in cultural matters can cause serious problems to international operations. The transfer of Western values to the East, for example, may be inappropriate, and corporate culture and management practices may need modifying to suit local conditions. Hofstede's work has provided a framework for understanding cultural differences.

2 _____

Hofstede defines culture as being collective, but often intangible. Nonetheless, it is what distinguishes one group, organisation, or nation from another. In his view, it is made up of two main elements: internal values, which are invisible, and external elements, which are more visible and are known as practices. The cultures of different organisations can be distinguished from one another by their practices, while national cultures can be differentiated by their values.

Values are among the first things that are programmed into children. These are reinforced by the local environment at school and at work. It is, therefore, difficult for an individual to change them in later life, and this is the reason why expatriate workers often experience difficulties when faced with another national culture.

3 _____

Hofstede is eager to emphasise that his 'dimensions' (or characteristics) are not a prescription or formula but merely a concept or framework. They equip us with an analytical tool to help us understand intercultural differences. All of Hofstede's dimensions represent two ends of a 'scale', for example the 'individualism/collectivism' dimension. In India, China and Japan, which are strong collectivist cultures, people need to belong to and have loyalty to a group. In other societies, such as the UK, individualism is more important and there is a lower emphasis on loyalty and protection. In strong collectivist countries, companies often have stronger obligations towards their employees and their families.

Multi-national companies building international teams, for instance, can make use of Hofstede's framework to make sense of the cultural differences they encounter in their practical experience. Knowing about such differences can help to avoid conflict in international management. Using the framework shows that it is not always safe to assume that apparently similar countries in the same region, for example Holland and Belgium or Austria and Hungary, have similar cultures.

4 _____

His framework has been used by other researchers to determine the suitability of certain management techniques for various countries or to make comparisons between countries to understand cultural differences in various areas of management.

Hofstede has also extended his work by collaborating with Henry Mintzberg, linking Mintzberg's five organisational structures with his own cultural dimensions. This link is intended to show that some organisational structures fit better in some national cultures than in others.

Source: *Business – The Ultimate Resource*

2 Read the article again and decide which section the following headings refer to.

a Dimensions in Practice
b Application and Collaboration
c Life and Career
d Key Thinking

3 According to the article, which of the following statements are true?

1 Geert Hofstede has worked at IBM for many years. _____
2 Now that business is more international, cultural sensitivity is extremely important. _____
3 We have to change our management style depending on the country we are in. _____
4 Different countries have different sets of values. _____
5 Hofstede's dimensions are a way to help us understand different cultures. _____
6 Hofstede has researched organisational cultures. _____

4 Find words or expressions in the article to match the following definitions.

1 being the first in a particular area (paragraph 1) _____
2 later or following (paragraph 1) _____
3 name used instead of the real one (paragraph 1) _____
4 include (paragraph 1) _____
5 something you cannot see or touch (paragraph 2) _____
6 strengthened (paragraph 3) _____
7 prepare, give the necessary skills to (paragraph 4) _____
8 find, come across (paragraph 5) _____
9 disagreement (paragraph 5) _____
10 being acceptable or right for someone or something (paragraph 6) _____

5 The following words can be confusing because they have similar meanings or because they are 'false friends'. Match the words with their definitions.

1	ignorance	**a**	show or find the difference between things which are compared
2	insensitivity	**b**	standard or accepted way of doing something, or a mathematical rule
3	distinguish	**c**	not aware of or showing sympathy for other people's feelings
4	differentiate	**d**	contain a number of different parts
5	prescription	**e**	not having enough knowledge about something
6	formula	**f**	a fixed way to solve a problem or a piece of paper on which a doctor writes the details of the medicine that someone needs
7	make up of	**g**	notice or understand the difference between two things, or to make one person or thing seem different from another

6 Complete the sentences with the correct form of the words from exercises 4 and 5.

1 We will _____ serious problems if a reduced budget causes us to change our winning _____s.
2 Unfortunately, his _____ to cultural issues often led to _____ in our overseas markets at sales conferences.
3 He's colour-blind and can't _____ the difference between red and green.
4 Many teenagers are surprisingly _____ about current events – if they just spent some time every day watching the news it would _____ them with a good general knowledge.
5 The committee is _____ representatives from every department.
6 We do not _____ between our employees on the basis of race or gender or any other issue.
7 I didn't realise that one of my colleagues actually writes thrillers, but he writes under a _____ .
8 The rain caused widespread flooding. The _____ road closures meant the town was cut off for three days.

Writing 3
Argument-led writing

1 Read the following short text about unions in the workplace and note the pros and cons under the following headings.

Arguments for unions

_____

_____

_____

Arguments against unions

_____

_____

_____

_____

Unions were originally set up to help workers negotiate collectively for wages and better conditions **since** individual employees had very little power or influence. **While** unions can help their members by negotiating better working conditions, they can sometimes raise benefits to unrealistically high levels. **As a result**, companies may have to increase product prices and this may lead to a fall in demand and possibly even job cuts. **Even though** unions can help to foster a sense of teamwork in the workplace, some argue that they create a hostile environment between managers and workers. Some governments and large corporations have tried to cut back on the unions' power **for the reason that** they have become too strong and have made it difficult for companies to react flexibly to changing markets.

2 Put the highlighted words from the text in exercise 1 into the correct columns in the table below. Then add some more words and phrases to each column. The first letters have been given to help you.

Present reasons	State result	Make a contrast
	s_____	
b_____	s_____	b_____
	t_____	
f_____	t_____	w_____
i_____		a_____
t_____		
s_____		h_____
a_____		

3 Complete the sentences with the phrases from the table in exercise 2. Some letters have been given to help you.

1 We need to increase our production _____ of rising demand.

2 A_____ most of our range is obsolete, this product is better than anything else on the market.

3 We've decided to give the whole team a bonus this year _____ _____ they have worked so hard.

4 Having a staff party is good for morale, _____ most members of staff are in favour of it.

5 The life cycle of the latest product is very short, w_____ some of the older products have lasted much longer.

6 The suppliers have put up the costs of our raw materials. _____ _____ _____ we have been forced to increase our prices.

7 Unfortunately, this site is still running at a loss, _____ _____ many cost-saving measures have been implemented.

8 Installing the new software has made the ordering process quicker _____ _____ there are now far fewer errors and orders are processed within two hours of receipt.

4 Write a short report on the pros and cons of one of the following topics (80–100 words).

1 Free public transport
2 Using renewable energy, such as wind or solar power
3 Making music downloads free
4 Privatisation of water supplies

Use the following outline from the Student's Book to help you:

- Introduction: introduce the topic; give background information
- Main body: Paragraph 1: outline and analyse pros,
  Paragraph 2: outline and analyse cons,
  Conclusion: summarise key points, state your conclusion

7 Change management

Idiomatic language

1 Complete the sentences by choosing the correct alternative from the words in brackets.

1 The team's enthusiasm for the marketing campaign petered _____ after a few months. (out / away / off)

2 Luckily there was a window _____ opportunity to resolve our differences at the meeting. (into / for / of)

3 The celebrity, who retired several years ago, has started to crave the _____ once more. (lamplight / spotlight / limelight)

4 We hope that the 'walking bus' idea for children will _____ root and spread throughout the country. (grow / take / get)

5 Having people _____ the coalface, speaking to the public, will help to get a clearer idea of market needs. (at / on / in front of)

6 The sales manager said it was gut-_____ to lose the contract, after all the effort they had put into trying to renew it. (pulling / breaking / wrenching)

7 The new CEO, who has a history of success tackling the _____ issues of business, will start next week at the troubled company. (sticky / thorny / prickly)

8 Unfortunately, the new project ran _____ trouble just a few weeks after it started, because of issues with the new product. (into / in / through)

2 Complete the sentences using the idioms from exercise 1.

1 We're keen for the new system to _____ and we're doing everything we can to promote it.

2 We need to get someone in who can _____ : someone who isn't afraid of dealing with the difficult problems the company is facing in this competitive market.

3 After a very long meeting, everyone was feeling tired and the conversation at dinner gradually _____ .

4 We have to face the _____ decision of which department will see the most job losses.

5 He had the chance to retire from professional sport last year, but he didn't because he still _____ .

6 The company _____ after demand for the product fell sharply, and they were left with too much stock.

7 The conference, with so many new product presentations, provided the perfect _____ to promote the new product.

8 Teachers who are _____ , working with the children, have doubts as to whether the system will work or not.

Cohesion and referencing

1 Match the two halves of the sentences.

1 More of the work will be done by robots,	a however, this is the first time we've had a chance to meet up socially.
2 Two different groups of people,	b and those actions have dramatically improved staff morale.
3 We've been working together for some time	c if the managers themselves are not aware of their employees' strengths, this won't work.
4 The new director has improved working conditions and increased bonuses	d thus fewer workers will be needed.
5 The leaders of both main political parties have called a meeting to discuss the issues	e the design team and the R&D department, are working on this project.
6 Managers should choose their own team leaders: that sounds reasonable, but	f and they assume that there will be some tough negotiating ahead.

2 Complete the text about change management with the correct linking phrase from exercise 1.

Companies often assume that the longer an initiative continues, the more likely it is to fail. **1** _____ , our studies show that a long-term project which is fully reviewed is more likely to succeed than a short-term one which isn't reviewed frequently enough. **2** _____ the time between reviews is more important than the length of the project. Reviewing and setting objectives are two very important stages in a project: **3** _____ _____ can determine its success or failure. Managers can sometimes feel that review meetings are a 'waste of time': **4** _____ _____ that the time could be better spent working on the project itself. **5** _____ _____ _____ _____ in fact, a short review meeting is an effective way to motivate the team. **6** _____ _____ _____ _____ _____ are usually involved in change projects – managers and their teams – and it's vital to get the backing of both before you proceed with new initiatives.

Present perfect simple and present perfect continuous

1 Complete the sentences by putting the verb in brackets in the correct tense.

1 You're very late for the meeting – we _____ for you for ages. (wait)

2 You must be starving, you _____ all day. (not eat)

3 They _____ the office since the new manager arrived and they've finally finished it! (redecorate)

4 We _____ to break into that market for years – maybe we'll do it with this new product. (try)

5 The new CEO _____ all employees to be aware of costs in these difficult economic conditions. (ask)

6 Do you think we're going to have the Christmas party? The new manager _____ anything about it. (not say)

2 Make complete sentences using these prompts.

Example: We/do/business with them for years and they/always pay/on time

Example: We've been doing business with them for years and they have always paid on time.

1 They / sell / the software for 15 years and they / not bring out / any updates.

_____

_____

2 We / develop / the product for several years but we still / not test / the prototype.

_____

_____

3 We / wait / for a reply from the patent office, but we / not hear / from them yet.

_____

_____

4 My boss / commute / from Scotland every week for the last two years and now he / just move / to London.

_____

_____

3 How could you say the following using either the present perfect simple or present perfect continuous?

Example: the company are offering a new service – ask how long

How _____ _____ _____

_____ _____ _____ the new service?

How long have/has the company been offering the new service?

1 the company are looking for a new Head Office – ask how long

How long _____ _____ _____

_____ _____ _____ a new Head Office?

2 ask the number of days' holiday taken this year

How _____ _____ _____

_____ _____ _____ this year?

3 say the employee made 6 sales since last week

You _____ _____ _____ _____

since last week.

4 the company have a new line of healthcare products – ask how long

How long _____ _____ _____

_____ the new line?

5 say the company started developing the new product last year and still is

The company _____ _____ _____ the

new product _____ _____ _____ .

6 ask the number of rooms booked for the conference

How _____ _____ _____

_____ _____ for the conference?

Skills

Review! ⊙

🎧 28–30 **Listen to tracks 28–30, which are from the Student's Book. Notice how the spoken language is structured in face-to-face negotiations and meetings using HBT structures.**

Organising spoken language – head, body, tail

1 Are the following words and expressions heads or tails? Put the words into the correct column, Head or Tail, depending on its function. Some expressions can be in both columns.

> I mean   you know   don't you   yeah (with rising intonation)
> well, yes, I see   doesn't it   you know what I mean
> as far as I'm concerned   I'm sorry to trouble you   I think
> right   OK (with rising intonation)   so   but
> as far as I'm concerned (up-down intonation)   yeah   erm
> basically   I see what you mean but   do you see what I mean
> in my opinion   right (with rising intonation)   OK
> well, I see what you mean but

Head	Tail

2 Complete the missing 'part' of the sentences with the head or tail structure. Some letters have been given to help you.

1 B_____ , it means how many markets have been out of stock for the period, r_____?

2 I_____ _____ _____ _____ but don't you think other factors are important too?

3 As far _____ _____ _____ , selling direct is interesting, but using agents may be possible too, do you s_____ _____ _____ _____?

4 _____ _____ we need to move on, _____ _____?

5 I m_____ we have to think of the costs, O_____?

6 So, y_____ _____ , the main difference is the level of cover, y_____ _____ _____ _____ m_____?

7 Y_____, it means we need to rethink the budget, _____ _____?

8 S_____ , you'll start working on that straight away, y_____?

3 Look at the following examples of the head, body, tail structure and mark the pauses with a | and the intonation at the end of each sentence with an arrow → .

Example: So | it's kind of more like just a pair of the right hands / isn't it?

1 You know there may be an alternative way of doing it you know what I mean?

2 Basically there's no black-and-white answer to that as far as I'm concerned.

3 Well I mean I would really welcome that if you see what I mean.

4 In my opinion that doesn't give us enough cover does it?

5 I see what you mean but I just think it's one of those things where they'll always find an excuse don't you?

6 So it doesn't necessarily mean we have to start again right?

7 Well I think we should go ahead with it OK?

8 Erm we need to get things started as soon as possible you know what I mean?

🎧 31 **Now listen and check your answers. Finally, listen again and try to match the model.**

CEF Can Do statements

Now you have completed the exercises in this unit, read the following statements. Tick the boxes that apply to you.

	Yes, I can do this.	I think I need more practice.
1 I can use some business idioms and the language of cohesion and referencing to structure language more effectively.	☐	☐
2 I can use and contrast the present perfect and present perfect continuous.	☐	☐
3 I can structure spoken language in face-to-face negotiations and meetings.	☐	☐

If you need more practice on points 1–3, check your Student's Book:

1 Lesson 7.1   2 Lesson 7.2   3 Lesson 7.3

Make a note of the areas you want to practise more and how you can do this.

8 Project management

Vocabulary and Grammar

Project stages

1 Look at the sentences describing different stages of project management. Replace the underlined words with a word or phrase with similar meaning. The first letters have been given to help you.

Example: At the trial stage, we test (p_____) the solution with real people.'

At the trial stage, we pilot the solution with real people.

1 In the detailed investigation stage, we do (u_____) a feasibility study of the options and define the chosen solution.

2 In the operation and closure phases, we implement the plan (p_____ i_____ i_____ p_____) and finally, close the project.

3 The first (i_____) investigation includes a short general view (b_____ o_____) of the possible needs (r_____) and solutions.

Now look at three more project stages. Put these stages, together with items 1–3, in the correct order.

4 Development and testing – build the solution
5 Proposal – identify the idea or need
6 Trial stage – pilot the solution with real people.

1 _____   4 _____
2 _____   5 _____
3 _____   6 _____

Verb/noun combinations for project planning

1 Complete the verb/noun collocations for project planning with the correct words.

1 screen out   u_ _ _ _ _ _ _ p_ _ _ _ _ _ _
2 engaging   t_ _ s_ _ _ _ _ _ _ _ _ _
3 encourage   t_ _ _ _ _ _ _
4 gather   i_ _ _ _ _ _ _ _
5 cut   c_ _ _ _
6 increase   c_ _ _ _ _ _ _ _ _
7 slash   d_ _ _ _ _ _ _ t_ _ _ _

Project stages

2 Complete the following 'Tips for Successful Projects' with the collocations from exercise 1.

1 Although you can't plan the whole project in detail from start to finish, you can _____ within each stage which will help you to plan the next part.

2 As the project continues, more detailed plans and better information will help to _____ amongst team members.

3 Taking longer in the investigative stages can be time well spent: for example, detailed research into the best ways to get the product to the market can mean a company is able to _____ .

4 Having a clear strategy makes it easier to _____ in the early stages so you don't waste time.

5 _____ is essential for the success of the project: if some people feel they haven't been consulted, the project could fail.

6 It is essential to _____ : frequent meetings and good communication amongst members will help with this.

7 Making changes in later stages of the project can be expensive and cause delays, so spending time in the early stages is beneficial and can often help to _____ .

Future perfect and future continuous

1 Read sentences 1–6 and decide what each one's function is. Put each sentence into the correct column of the table on page 37.

1 We'll be developing the new prototype in March next year.

2 The company will have already opened offices in Hong Kong and Singapore by next June.

3 At this rate, we'll still be building the factory when we should be producing the first new models!

4 By the time he graduates, he'll have already spent more than 20 years in full-time education!

5 I don't think I'll have finished the report in time for the meeting – what do you think I should do?

6 Unfortunately they've closed the Italian restaurant next to the office, so we won't be having any more business lunches there.

<table>
<tr><td>To talk about something in progress in the future (or expected to be in progress in the future)</td><td>To talk about something that is seen as already completed before a certain time</td></tr>
</table>

To talk about something in progress in the future (or expected to be in progress in the future)	To talk about something that is seen as already completed before a certain time

2 Complete sentences 1–8 with the correct form of the verb in brackets, using the future perfect or future perfect continuous.

1 Can you make sure you've sent over all the information as they _____ the figures this afternoon? (go through)

2 Despite the technical problems, I hope we _____ all the applications for the new post by the closing date. (receive)

3 I don't think the Board _____ their decision by the time we have the AGM. It's a very complicated problem to resolve. (announce)

4 In spite of the difficult financial conditions, we _____ the computer system in the next 2 months. (fully upgrade)

5 Over the coming year the company _____ heavily in new plant and equipment in order to modernise the factory. (invest)

6 We hope we _____ the new reporting system by the beginning of the next financial year. (set up)

7 All of the sales team _____ full training on the new product range during the next quarter. (undergo)

8 Do you think you _____ the problem by the time I get back? (sort out)

3 Look at the Gantt chart showing the project stages for the building of a new sports stadium. It is now August. Complete the missing time phrases in sentences 1–7 below.

Project Activity	This year					Next year							
	Aug	Sep	Oct	Nov	Dec	Jan	Feb	Mar	Apr	May	Jun	Jul	Aug
	▓	dig foundations				▓	complete running track						
		▓	pour concrete					▓	dig swimming pool				
	erect stands		▓	▓									
									put on roof	▓			
									install seats		▓	▓	
										finish project			▓

1 _____ _____ _____ of this month we will have dug the foundations.

2 _____ _____ _____ month we will be pouring the concrete.

3 _____ 2 _____ _____ we'll be erecting the stands.

4 _____ _____ _____ of January we will have completed the running track.

5 _____ 6 _____ _____ we'll be digging the swimming pool.

6 _____ _____ _____ of June we will have put on the roof.

7 _____ _____ _____ time the whole project will be finished!

Skills

Review! ⊙

🎧 32 Listen to track 32, which is from the Student's Book. Notice how the speaker uses indirect language to maintain a good business relationship in their meeting.

Signalling identities through 'we'

1 🎧 34 The project managers (Ron and Dev) of a sports stadium are meeting with their business sponsors (Torsten and Sylvia). Listen to part of the meeting and complete the gaps.

Ron: So, we've been going through the schedules and **1** _____ _____ _____ _____ _____ a bit more time to complete the project. I mean, we're not …

Torsten: But I thought **2** _____ _____ _____ the last time we met and you said that was the last extension you'd be asking for.

Ron: Look, **3** _____ _____ _____ _____ _____ to be a success …

Sylvia: Yes, and we don't want our name associated with something which isn't absolutely top quality …

Dev: 4 _____ _____ _____!

Sylvia: … so what I was going to say was, maybe we shouldn't worry so much about a couple of extra weeks as long as we **5** _____ _____ _____ to the highest specifications.

Ron: You're right: and of course we don't want to overrun by months as **6** _____ _____ _____ _____ the grand opening …

Torsten: OK, how about the costs – what **7** _____ _____ _____ _____ _____ – are we going to be massively over our budget?

Dev: I don't think so – the sub-contractors are on a fixed price, so the extra time shouldn't impact on the price and if **8** _____ _____ _____ _____ _____ _____ _____ on them, I'm sure we can get it down to a couple of weeks, maximum …

Sylvia: OK, because we can't **9** _____ _____ _____ any further …

Ron: And we wouldn't want you to – we really value your sponsorship and I think **10** _____ _____ _____ really well so far …

2 Sort the sentences you have completed in exercise 1 into the different uses of 'we' listed below.

a Exclusive present / corporate 'we' _____

b Inclusive present / corporate 'we' _____

c Vague 'we' _____

3 Look at the following sentences from the sales meeting in 8.3 of the Student's Book and decide which type of 'we/us' is being used. Charles and Liam are from an IT company and they are talking to Valentina, their client.

1 Valentina: Right. OK. That might be a cheaper thing for <u>us</u> to do.

2 Liam: And I'm sure with all this stuff there's a way of doing it where it's going to please <u>us</u> all.

3 Valentina: Just fit them in around what else you do. But it's just useful information for <u>us</u>.

4 Liam: And I think <u>we</u>'ve got a football match the week after next, haven't <u>we</u>?

5 Liam: So <u>we</u> need to get those figures to you. <u>We</u> should be able to get those to you this afternoon or tomorrow.

6 Liam: And then you know, <u>we</u>'ll perhaps wait for you to come back to <u>us</u> about the next stage.

a Exclusive present / corporate 'we' _____

b Inclusive present / corporate 'we' _____

c Vague 'we' _____

CEF Can Do statements

Now you have completed the exercises in this unit, read the following statements. Tick the boxes that apply to you.

	Yes, I can do this.	I think I need more practice.
1 I can use key vocabulary to talk about project management.	☐	☐
2 I can use future perfect and future continuous tenses.	☐	☐
3 I can recognise the different uses of 'we'.	☐	☐

If you need more practice on points 1–3, check your Student's Book:

1 Lesson 8.1   **2** Lesson 8.2   **3** Lesson 8.3

Make a note of the areas you want to practise more and how you can do this.

What would Peter Say?

Listening to the wisdom of Peter Drucker might have helped us avoid – and will help us solve – numerous challenges plaguing communities around the world: restoring trust in business in the wake of accounting scandals and the global financial crisis; attracting and motivating the best talent without creating crippling financial commitments; addressing societal problems such as climate change, health care, and public education.

If Peter Drucker were here today, what would he have to say about such important matters? His first comment might be 'I told you so' – and he would have every right to say that. He took a broad look at the context surrounding organisations, noting jarring events he called discontinuities. Next, since the signs of difficulties ahead were there all along, he might follow up by telling us, 'Look at the underlying systems'. Then he might finish by asking leaders a few thought-provoking questions: 'What is your mission? What should you stop doing? Where has the drive for short-term efficiencies undermined long-term effectiveness? What should be your objectives and guiding principles?'

Drucker's extraordinary ability to spot trends and predict impending problems was not magic. He put business in the context of society, and he saw society as increasingly composed of organisations with a wide range of goals. By looking at all types rather than specialising in a few, he could view the inter-dependencies and discover the implications of small changes in one area for activities in another area.

Here are some of the critical issues Drucker anticipated:

1 _____

Drucker would not have been surprised that incentives to take excessive risks contributed to the recent global financial meltdown. Back in the mid-1980s, he warned about a public outcry over executive compensation – a main theme on the US government's agenda following the fall of banks in 2008.

2 _____

At a time when changes are happening quickly, there are more opportunities for entrepreneurs to create and transform organisations. They need to be ahead of the changes in society, as Drucker said 'the best way to predict the future is to invent it.' For example a company like General Motors could not just survive by doing the same things with improved efficiency and lower costs, it needed to reorganise the way it thought and its company structure.

3 _____

Drucker warned that competition from emerging markets would eventually challenge the United States' global economic dominance. Not surprisingly, Drucker is a hero in emerging countries. He helped leaders in those nations to move from family-based enterprises to professional management. This paved the way for companies that could grow and compete in international markets.

4 _____

Drucker focused on how organisations could best achieve their purpose, not on business per se or on profit as the main indicator of success. He felt that business could learn from the not-for-profit sector about sources of motivation that lay beyond a financial bottom line.

Guidance for the future

What would Peter say about the path forward a century after his birth? To restore trust in business, he would ask managers to become self-regulating rather than stand by and risk over-regulation. He would applaud the few courageous CEOs who are setting limits on their own pay.

For improvement in health care or education he would look at entire systems, including community organisations, and he would encourage government, business and civil society to cooperate in change. For international collaboration on global warming and other environmental issues, he would ask government leaders to think beyond sovereignty to define a common sense of purpose.

Drucker was not a revolutionary. He merely asked that we constantly challenge assumptions. He recognised that leading in turbulent times requires foresight about where things are heading as well as judgment about what not to change.

Source: *Harvard Business Review*, by Rosabeth Moss Kanter

1 Look at the summaries of the critical issue paragraphs 1, 2 and 3 and the 'Guidance for the future' section of the text, and match them with the correct paragraph.

a Drucker said there were more opportunities for people in changing times, but they have to be ahead of the changes. _____

b Drucker did not just concentrate on businesses and profit, but also on organisations in other sectors. _____

c Drucker predicted some of the problems we are suffering from today. _____

d Drucker predicted the rising influence of developing countries, where his ideas are very popular. _____

2 Drucker anticipated the following four key issues. Match them with the four spaces in the text.

a Auto industry troubles and creativity in difficult times
b The new economic powers
c The not-for-profit sector
d The bonus controversy

3 Look at the following words and decide if they have a positive or negative meaning in the text.

	Positive	Negative
1 plaguing (paragraph 1)		
2 crippling (paragraph 1)		
3 jarring (paragraph 2)		
4 undermined (paragraph 2)		
5 impending (paragraph 3)		
6 restore (paragraph 8)		
7 applaud (paragraph 8)		
8 turbulent (paragraph 10)		

4 Match the words from exercise 3 with the correct definition.

1 plaguing	a became less effective
2 crippling	b bring back
3 jarring	c unsettled / involving a lot of sudden changes
4 undermined	d causing difficulty
5 impending	e praise
6 restore	f severely damaging / making sth weak
7 applaud	g seeming wrong or unsuitable
8 turbulent	h something that will happen soon

5 Look at the following expressions from the text and match the 2 parts.

1 financial	a outcry
2 in the	b way for
3 bottom	c meltdown
4 public	d line
5 pave the	e wake of

6 Now match the expressions 1–5 from exercise 5 with the correct definitions a–e.

a angry expression of protest or shock _____

b sudden and complete failure of a system _____

c create a situation that makes it easier for something to happen _____

d happening after an event or as a result of it _____

e the amount of money that a business makes or loses _____

7 Complete the sentences with the expressions from exercises 3 and 5.

1 After a _____ year as CEO, with many difficulties, he finally stepped down when there was a _____ over his bonus and salary level.

2 The Prime Minister has to move quickly to _____ confidence after this scandal – just the latest in a long line of problems which have been _____ the government.

3 The new regulations were introduced _____ the banking crisis which had _____ confidence in the government's ability to deal with the situation.

4 The agreement will _____ for more trade between the two countries.

5 I think we should _____ the decision to improve working conditions, even if it means more expense.

Writing 4
Describing graphs

1 Look at the graph below which shows unemployment levels in the US between January 1980 and January 2010 and decide if the sentences are true (T) or false (F).

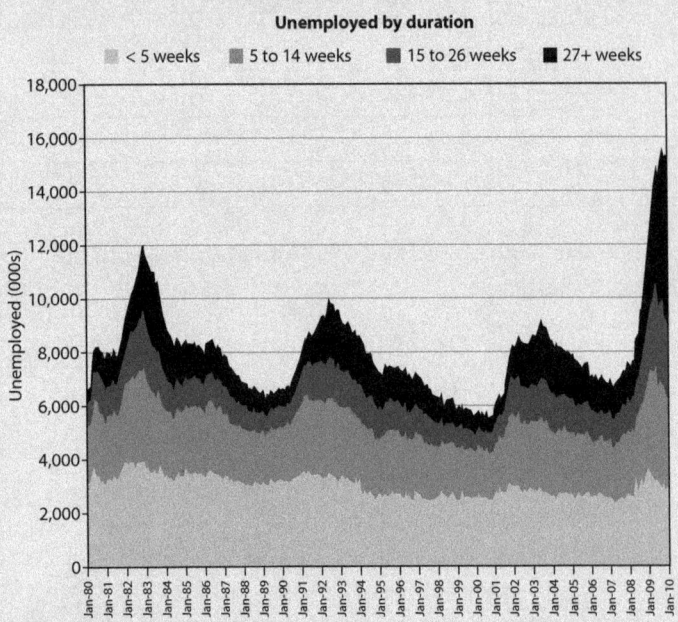

Unemployed by duration

▨ < 5 weeks   ▨ 5 to 14 weeks   ▦ 15 to 26 weeks   ■ 27+ weeks

5 weeks = short-term unemployed   5 to 14 weeks = short/medium-term unemployed
15 to 26 weeks = medium-term unemployed   27+ weeks = long-term unemployed

1 The level of short-term unemployed has remained fairly constant over the whole period. _____

2 Between January 1982 and 1983, medium-term unemployment rose slightly. _____

3 There were more long-term unemployed between January 1985 and January 1987 than short/medium-term unemployed during the same time. _____

4 Long-term unemployment shows much greater peaks than short-term unemployment. _____

Comparisons and contrasts

2 Complete the expressions in the sentences below based on the unemployment graph in exercise 1. Some letters have been given to help you.

1 The level of unemployment was v_____ 16 million in January 2010.

2 The levels of long-term unemployment show c_____ different trends to those of short-term unemployment.

3 Between January 1988 and 1990, the totals of short- and short/medium-term unemployed was t_____ d_____ to the totals for the longer-term unemployed.

4 In the last year shown on the graph, the long-term unemployment level is a g_____ d_____ higher than any of the other levels shown.

5 The level of medium-term unemployment between January 1981 and 1982 is almost e_____ the s_____ a_____ the level between January 1986 to 1987.

3 Look at the <u>underlined</u> mistakes below, about the graph in exercise 1, and correct them. Some of the mistakes are language mistakes and some are about the content of the graph.

1 The peak in January 2010 is <u>totally</u> the highest on the graph. _____

2 Between January 2003 and 2004, long-term unemployment levels were <u>quite</u> higher than medium-term levels. _____

3 The level of unemployment between 1980 and 1982 is <u>exactly</u> the same as between 1984 and 1985. _____

4 Overall, the long-term unemployment levels are <u>totally</u> different from the medium-term levels. _____

4 Look at the graph below which shows house prices and the value of housing stock (the total number of residential units available) in New Zealand between 1990 and 2010. Write a short summary (about 150 words) of the key information including some comparisons. Use the outline given below to help you.

Paragraph 1: A general description of the graph
Paragraph 2: Explanation of what is in the graph, starting with comparisons of general trends, moving to comparisons of specific points
Paragraph 3: A one-sentence conclusion that summarises the general trend in the graph

House prices and value of housing stock

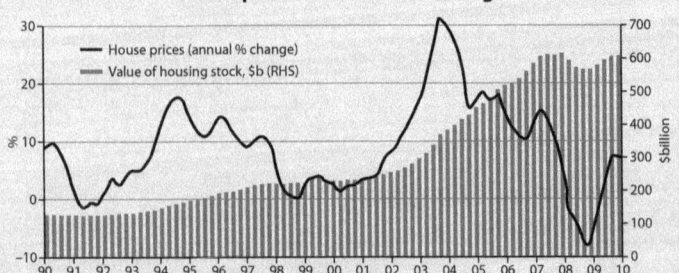

9 E-marketing

Vocabulary and Grammar

Marketing and e-marketing terms

1 Complete the description of the 4Ps/4Cs theories.

The traditional combination of the 4Ps was known as the

1 m_____ **2** m_____ . These factors looked at

marketing from the **3** p_____ perspective. A more recent

theory is the 4Cs which looks at marketing from the

4 c_____ perspective.

Each of the 4Ps relates to one of the 4Cs. **5** P_____ (what

companies charge) can been seen as **6** c_____ to the

customer (the amount customers will actually pay).

7 P_____ (what is being sold) can be seen as customer

8 w_____ and **9** n_____ (what the customer is

interested in). **10** P_____ (where it is sold) can be seen

as **11** c_____ to the customer (recognising customer's

choice and ease of buying) and **12** p_____ (ways in which

companies persuade customers to buy) can be seen as

13 c_____ with the customer (a two-way process involving

feedback from customers).

2 Use the clues to find the words. The first letters have been given to help you.

1 A company which only has online stores (e.g. Amazon).

e-_____ (7 letters)

2 A company which only has online stores. p_____

p_____ (4, 4 letters)

3 A company which has both online and high-street stores.

b_____ and c_____ operator. (6, 6 letters)

4 A company which has both online and high-street stores.

m_____-c_____ retailer (5, 7 letters)

5 A computer program which finds information on the Internet

(e.g. Google). s_____ e_____ (6, 6 letters)

6 A type of marketing which helps companies create new media
campaigns using blogs and social network sites to communicate
with their customers. s_____ m_____
(6, 5 letters)

7 Something that can be done or seen using a computer, without
going anywhere or talking to anyone. v_____ (7 letters)

8 A large amount of information stored in a computer system in
such a way that it can be easily looked at or changed.
d_____ (8 letters)

3 Choose the best word to complete each gap from the alternatives given on page 43.

StrikeSports

StrikeSports was set up in 1985 as a
1 _____ selling sports clothing and equipment.
There were **2** _____ in several major cities
where customers could browse and buy. As the internet
grew and the number of **3** _____ increased, the
company opened a **4** _____ **StrikeSports.com**
to sell its products alongside its **5** _____ . This
side of the business has grown dramatically and Strike
Sports is constantly looking for new ways to reach its
6 _____ . The company uses **7** _____ to
analyse online customer feedback and they have worked
with consultants to achieve better **8** _____ –
making the website easier to navigate. Recently, it
has become more involved with **9** _____ with
the introduction of a loyalty card to learn more about
customers' shopping habits and preferences. With both a
strong High Street presence and website, Strike Sports
is a true **10** _____ .

1 **A** dot.com	**B** bricks retailer	**C** warehouse
2 **A** retail outlets	**B** localities	**C** physical places
3 **A** physical stores	**B** dot.coms	**C** pure plays
4 **A** search engine	**B** retailer	**C** virtual store
5 **A** physical stores	**B** retailers	**C** wholesalers
6 **A** clients	**B** shoppers	**C** target consumers
7 **A** data handling	**B** database marketing	**C** e-marketing
8 **A** web browsing	**B** web optimisation	**C** search engine optimisation
9 **A** customer interaction	**B** customer relations	**C** customer relationship marketing
10 **A** multi-player	**B** multi-channel retailer	**C** e-tailer

Standard and mixed conditionals

1 Match the two halves of the sentences.

1 We would have launched the new product earlier	**a** if there's a problem with the product.
2 The company will start selling through retailers	**b** if they had set up an e-tailing operation earlier.
3 We always contact customers directly	**c** if we'd known what the competition were doing.
4 They would attract younger customers	**d** if they had started the new campaign last month.
5 The company would be in a stronger position today	**e** if we can get established in the Asian market.
6 We could have given the customers a more personalised service	**f** if they were willing to pay more.
7 We'll be ahead of the competition	**g** if they had a presence on social networking sites.
8 They wouldn't have to rely on the retail outlets so heavily	**h** if the market research shows that's what customers want.

2 Complete the gaps with the correct form of the verb in brackets.

1 If the company decides to close down all its stores and become a dot.com pure play, it _____ (mean) a lot of staff redundancies.

2 If we _____ (follow) the consultants' advice last year, we wouldn't be in this situation.

3 If you only use the 4Ps of the marketing mix, you _____ (not consider) the customer's perspective.

4 They _____ (not spend) so much on development if they hadn't received positive feedback on the prototype.

5 The company would need to set up an e-retail shop if they _____ (want) to become a multi-channel retailer.

6 Customers won't find it easy to navigate the website unless we _____ (improve) the layout.

7 If we were registered with more search engines, we _____ (might have) more hits last month.

8 Unless we _____ (ask) our customers for feedback last month, we wouldn't have realised the potential problems with the products.

Skills

🔊 34–35 Listen to tracks 34–35, which are from the Student's Book. Notice how the speaker structures his e-presentation, and in particular any phrases used to introduce slides.

Delivering an e-presentation

1 Look at the first part of the script from Philip Weiss's e-presentation. First, mark the sentence breaks using a full stop (.). Then, think about where you would pause for effect and mark each pause with a /.

> Hi my name is Philip Weiss and I'm the managing director of Zn over the next five minutes I'll give you a brief introduction of who we are how we can help HQs meet their challenges and what opportunities the Internet created for them and how we developed a methodology to think differently and execute online campaigns and finally we'll look at how we can help you.

🔊 34 Listen to track 34 again and check your answers. Practise saying it with the correct pauses.

Introducing and linking slides

1 In his presentation, Philip Weiss uses rhetorical questions to engage the audience. Look at the following two examples from track 35 and mark the stress and intonation – where does his voice go up and down?

So what are the main challenges facing HQs today?

So how can we help you?

Mark the stress and intonation on the following rhetorical questions.

1 How many of you here today have tried this product?

2 Does this problem sound familiar?

3 What is the biggest challenge we're facing today?

4 So how could we solve this problem?

5 Where will our next big market be?

6 So what's the secret of their success?

🔊 36 Now listen and check your answers.

Finally, listen and repeat. Try to match your intonation to the model.

2 Having a clear structure to a presentation is very important. Complete the following phrases for introducing and linking different topics within a presentation.

1 Over the next five minutes, I'll g_____ you a
  b_____ introduction of …

2 First let's l_____ a_____ …

3 Now let's t_____ t_____ …

4 M_____ o_____ now to …

5 The w_____ we s_____ our work is to …

6 We f_____ specifically o___ …

7 Finally, I'd like to t_____ a_____ …

8 If you're i_____ in pursuing this conversation,
  we l_____ f_____ to hearing from you.

3 Below is a slide from a presentation on e-marketing. Use the phrases from exercise 2 to introduce and move from one topic to the next.

Example: Over the next five minutes, I'll give you a brief introduction to e-marketing …

E-Marketing

- Marketing concept
- E-market planning
- Competitor analysis
- Objective setting

🔊 37 Listen to the model and check your pronunciation and intonation.

CEF Can Do statements

Now you have completed the exercises in this unit, read the following statements. Tick the boxes that apply to you.

	Yes, I can do this.	I think I need more practice.
1 I can use marketing and e-marketing terms to discuss business concepts.	☐	☐
2 I can use mixed conditionals and standard conditionals to talk about past, present and future possibilities.	☐	☐
3 I can give a simple, prepared presentation on a marketing or business-related topic.	☐	☐

If you need more practice on points 1–3, check your Student's Book:

1 Lesson 9.1   2 Lesson 9.2   3 Lesson 9.3

Make a note of the areas you want to practise more and how you can do this.

10 Branding

Branding expressions

1 Find 4 words which can go before 'brand' and 4 words which can go after it and put them in the spaces. Some letters have been given to help you.

1 o_____

2 m_____

3 lu_____

4 li_____

(brand)

5 i_____

6 a_____

7 p_____

8 ex_____

2 Look at this extract from a presentation by the marketing manager of a frozen food company and complete the gaps using the expressions relating to branding from exercise 1.

As you know, our main target for this year is to improve our brand **1** _____ as we feel most consumers haven't heard of us, and we are not well-known in our target market. Although we produce a lot of frozen food products for the supermarkets, this is labelled as their **2** _____ brand, so our name is not recognised as a **3** _____ brand. The brand **4** _____ we'd like to project is one of quality and also good value for money, so not a **5** _____ brand at present. We're also thinking about brand **6** _____ – how will our brand fit in with the competition? What are the main benefits of buying our product? We feel, as our brand becomes more well-known, we could look at some brand **7** _____ , perhaps moving into other frozen foods, frozen fruit and vegetables for example. If this is successful, we could even look at offering this as a **8** _____ brand for other companies to produce for us. However, that's a long way off and would probably give us the possibility to do some further brand **9** _____ to open up new market sectors. As I said, our main focus at present is to make sure more people recognise our name and this will have the added benefit of raising our brand **10** _____ – how much the customers value our brand, how well they know us and want to choose our products over our competitors.

Describing brands and products

1 Complete the sentences with the words below.

extensions   assets   gross revenues   boost   beyond
attributed to   transmit   perceptions

1 Television advertising is the best way to _____ the image of the brand to our target audience.

2 Texas Instruments was able to cut its customer waiting time, which improved customer _____ of poor service.

3 Online marketing has led to McMahon increasing its _____ by 3 percent over the last six months.

4 Our latest marketing campaign aims to go _____ the basic features and emphasise the real lifestyle benefits of the product.

5 One of their biggest _____ is the customer base they have built up through marketing campaigns.

6 The brand's strength can be _____ the traditional values and luxury lifestyle that it represents.

7 We see our brands as _____ of our products – they represent our company in the marketplace.

8 The new group has made brands available exclusively for the Chinese market, which should _____ sales.

2 Use the clues to find the words.

1 Relating to things you can see or touch. _____ (8 letters)

2 Not expensive. _____ (10 letters)

3 Relating to or representing a set of beliefs or a way of life. _____ (6 letters)

4 Energetic, exciting and full of enthusiasm. _____ (7 letters)

5 Feeling happy and comfortable. _____ (7 letters)

6 Simple, without a lot of extra decoration. _____ (13 letters)

7 Making you feel hopeful or encouraged. _____ (13 letters)

8 Able to be used for many different purposes. _____ (9 letters)

3 Look at the following advertisement for a new range of clothing. Choose the best word for each gap from the choices below.

Our new range of eveningwear is full of vibrant
1 _____ which will lift your mood on those cold
winter nights. The range has plenty of variety, offering
you 2 _____ and inspirational 3 _____
which allow you to 'mix and match' so you can make lots
of outfits from just a few items. Add to any of the outfits
with our matching range of accessories – belts, jewellery
etc. to 'dress up' or 'dress down' for any occasion. The
pieces have a 4 _____ and 5 _____ which
will look just as good in a sophisticated restaurant or
night club as dining in with friends. What's more, we
haven't forgotten your 6 _____ – we know you
want to look and feel great wearing our clothes – that's
why they come in a wide range of sizes to suit everyone.
Last, but not least, our style is 7 _____ – prices
start from just €55. So, go ahead – treat yourself to this
8 _____ from City. We know you'll find the
perfect option for your perfect look this winter.

4 In each sentence there is one incorrect word. <u>Underline</u> the incorrect word and write the correct form at the end of the sentence.

1 Our latest swimwear designs were inspired from the fabrics and colours of the Orient. _____

2 The fabric ropes on our sandals are hard-wearing and comfortable. _____

3 The base texture of the shoe is based on the rice grain format. _____

4 The shoe's distinctive shape and strong emphasis on comfort are its unquestionable features. _____

1 A pleasure	**B** colours	**C** look
2 A versatile	**B** changeable	**C** efficient
3 A combinations	**B** pleasure	**C** feelings
4 A versatile	**B** efficient	**C** relaxed
5 A uncomplicated comfort	**B** uncomplicated style	**C** basic style
6 A physical clothes	**B** physical style	**C** physical comfort
7 A priceless	**B** valuable	**C** affordable
8 A iconic look	**B** iconic comfort	**C** versatile spirit

Skills

Review! 👁

🎧 **38** Listen to track 38, which is from the Student's Book. Notice how the manager uses language to direct and persuade her staff.

The language of persuasion

1 Look at the following sentences. First, underline the stressed words and then mark the pauses with a | . Remember, pausing can be powerful and persuasive.

Example: We don't just offer any service. We offer the best service.

Example: We don't just offer any service. | We offer the best service.

1 This is not just a good team. This is a fantastic team.

2 Yes, we want the business, but we need to deliver on time.

3 The product won't be an average product. It will be a superb product.

4 This is not just ordinary customer service. This is excellent customer service.

5 Yes, the deadline is important, but quality is more important.

6 This is no ordinary sales campaign, this is revolutionary.

7 People don't just buy our products for what they do, they're buying a lifestyle.

8 Yes, we want to be first in the market, but not if the quality suffers.

🎧 **39** Now, listen and check your answers. Finally, listen and try to match the model.

Using *if* to persuade and direct staff

1 Look at the following sentences and put them in the table according to how *if* is being used.

if to be conditional	*if* to persuade / direct

1 We can't produce any more if we don't have enough raw materials.

2 If you could try to keep your work area tidy, it would be appreciated.

3 If I walk into reception, I want to see someone there to welcome me.

4 If you see Johan, tell him I've finished.

5 If I'm talking to customers, I always use 'Mr' or 'Mrs'.

6 If we don't hurry up, we're not going to be ready on time.

7 They'd replace the equipment if they had a bigger budget.

8 I always try to sound polite and friendly if I'm dealing with customers.

2 Change the written instructions into 2 possible spoken forms, using *if*.

Example: Staff need to use the company name when they answer the phone.

a If you answer the phone, you need to use the company name.
b If I'm answering the phone, I always use the company name.

1 Staff need to greet visitors when they are working on the front desk.

a If you're _____ , _____ .
b If I'm _____ , _____ .

2 The sales team need to emphasise the benefits when they are selling a new product.

a If you're _____ , _____ .
b If I'm _____ , _____ .

3 The customer services team need to check the customer is happy when they make a follow-up call.

a If you're _____ , _____ .
b If I'm _____ , _____ .

4 Staff need to book the room in advance when they are arranging a meeting.

a If you're _____ , _____ .
b If I'm _____ , _____ .

🎧 **40** Now listen and check your answers.

CEF Can Do statements

Now you have completed the exercises in this unit, read the following statements. Tick the boxes that apply to you.

	Yes, I can do this.	I think I need more practice.
1 I can use a range of expressions and vocabulary to describe brands and products.	☐	☐
2 I can use appropriate language to persuade and direct people in business situations.	☐	☐

If you need more practice on points 1–2, check your Student's Book:

1 Lesson 10.1, 10.2   **2** Lesson 10.3

Make a note of the areas you need to practise more and how to do this.

On Writing as an Essential Business Skill

Why words matter

Words are the essential tools of communication. But they are so much more. They convey information, they express emotion; they influence, persuade, motivate. They do all the things that a successful business wants to do – if they are used well. Or, if they are used badly, they undermine a business.

Verbal identity

Many businesses, particularly those that follow principles of branding, now attach equal importance to words and images. Visual identity – the consistent use of logos, colours, typefaces, photography – is an established management procedure. Verbal identity – managing a brand's tone of voice through style, vocabulary, names – is in its relative infancy. Combining the visual and the verbal provides a way of making brands that really work. A prime objective of any modern brand is to create better relationships with its consumers. Companies use their brands to create and maintain better relationships through conversations, many of which take place in written form, whether in print, in emails or on the Internet. The words used in those conversations are reflections of a brand's personality. When products and services are basically similar, words can be the principal means of differentiating one company from another.

A case study

In 1998 three college friends formed a company that makes fruit smoothies. A very simple business and, at that time, a tiny market for the product. They called the company Innocent Drinks. They had little money to spend on visual identity, but the founders had a playful approach to words. They channelled their creative effort into writing words – humorous little stories – that appeared on the labels of their products.

Innocent's verbal identity begins with its name. They are innocent in the sense of being the little guys up against big corporations – but also in believing in the natural goodness of pure fruit, with no nasty (artificial/unnatural) additives. All their words reinforce this proposition through the disarming use of humour. A very clear sense of the Innocent personality emerges through every word they use, even down to a distinctive, honest but funny way of listing the ingredients of their products:

> **Ingredients** (strawberry and banana smoothie)
> 10 <u>pressed</u> apples, 27 <u>crushed</u> strawberries, 2½ <u>mashed</u> bananas, some freshly squeezed orange juice and <u>nothing else)</u>

The news about Innocent spread, appropriately enough, by word of mouth. People talked about them, shared the humour of the labels (which changed constantly) and became loyal fans. Innocent got other things right too, particularly distribution. In a few years they were everywhere, the United Kingdom's fastest-growing food and drink company.

Words are tricky

Many businesses have since tried to copy Innocent, but Innocent's success is built on the consistency of its tone of voice. It is relatively easy to manufacture a tone of voice that works in external communication such as advertising. But there is a danger if a brand's advertising sends one message and if a consumer's experience is completely different.

The individuality of words

A brand's tone of voice needs to work from the inside outwards, if it is to have real credibility. If a brand such as Apple promises to 'Think different', for example, this places responsibility on the behaviour of everyone representing the brand. The consumer has a right to expect a degree of creativity from all the brand's representatives.

Creativity is fundamental

Fifty years ago, 'creativity' was required only in an advertising agency. Today every business needs to be creative and it needs to inspire and harness the creativity of all its people. This is not an optional extra, but an essential requirement for survival, growth and reinvention. Businesses that lack creativity will increasingly struggle to survive. Creative skills therefore need to be encouraged and developed in businesses of all kinds. By developing people to express themselves more creatively through words, businesses can unlock the potential of innovation, increase the impact of communication and become more effective in winning business.

Source: *Business: The Ultimate Resource*

1 Read the text and decide which of the following sentences is the best summary.

1 Words are the most important marketing tool and if used wrongly they can damage business. _____

2 Creativity helps companies build relationships with their customers. _____

3 Innocent is an example of a company which uses visual identity very effectively. _____

4 Words and pictures are equally important in presenting the brand. _____

2 Read the article again. Are the statements true (T) or false (F)?

1 Visual identity includes the brand's tone of voice. _____

2 Words can help differentiate similar brands. _____

3 The founders of Innocent spent a lot of money on visual identity. _____

4 The name 'Innocent' reflects the founders' beliefs. _____

5 Companies have to make sure that the tone of voice which they use in their advertising is the same as the customer's experience of the brand. _____

6 Employees have to use the same words as found in the company's advertising. _____

7 Creativity should be developed at every level in the company to help businesses survive and grow. _____

3 Complete the expressions from the text with a preposition from the box. There are three prepositions you need to use twice.

with	in	of	from	by	on

1 the objective _____ (paragraph 2)

2 _____ print, _____ the Internet (paragraph 2)

3 differentiate _____ (paragraph 2)

4 begin _____ (paragraph 4)

5 to believe _____ (paragraph 4)

6 _____ word _____ mouth* (paragraph 5)

7 built _____ (paragraph 6)

* when people find out about an event, product or service by hearing about it from others who have had a positive experience.

4 Match the expressions from the text with the correct meaning.

1 convey (information)	a individual
2 channel (effort into)	b to experience difficulty and make a great effort to do something
3 reinforce	c comes across, becomes clear
4 emerges	d to communicate
5 distinctive	e to release, realise or make more active
6 consistency	f to control something in order to use its power
7 credibility	g to direct something into a particular place or situation
8 harness (the creativity)	h when something or someone can be believed or trusted
9 struggle	i not varied, always happening in the same way
10 unlock (the potential)	j to strengthen, back up

5 Complete the sentences with the expressions from exercises 3 and 4. You may need to change the form of the words.

1 We hope the image that _____ from our advertising in the media (both _____ _____ and _____ _____ _____) is one of traditional quality and value.

2 The main _____ _____ our advertising campaign is to _____ our position as market leader.

3 We want to _____ all our efforts into creating a brand that people can _____ _____ .

4 It's important to _____ ourselves _____ the competition.

5 Our company philosophy _____ _____ our staff: they represent us and our values and we hope they _____ a positive image to our customers.

6 After the recent problems with quality, the company is going to _____ to maintain its _____ – the customers may no longer trust them.

Writing 5
Persuasive communication online

The language of advertising

1 Complete the gaps with the correct words. The first letters have been given to help you.

1 Although we don't expect customers to take this product particularly seriously, it p_____ t_____ 'need for recognition' b_____ .

2 The first page of our promotion brochure has a section t_____ , 'Our philosophy'.

3 Customers b_____ i_____ these 'healthy living' ideas because they want to feel good about themselves.

4 Buying this product will give you p_____ o_____ benefits, including saving you time and money.

5 Advertisers often think about the benefits of a product, and what human need it will f_____ .

Changing features into benefits

1 Complete the gaps using the correct connecting phrases.

1 Our shampoo is enriched with extra vitamins, _____ _____ silky, shinier hair.

2 This product is more energy-efficient than anything else on the market _____ _____ that you save money on your energy bills.

3 Our phone lines are open 24 hours a day _____ _____ _____ _____ _____ _____ contact us whenever you have a question.

4 This new e-account pays a great rate of interest and is accessible online _____ _____ _____ check your balance whenever you want.

5 We offer the fastest internet speeds _____ that downloading films and music will be completed in seconds.

6 All our holidays are insured by one of the biggest companies in the world _____ _____ _____ peace of mind should anything go wrong.

2 Use the prompts to change these features into benefits.

Example: Olympus camera – lightweight, strong body – easy and safe to carry anywhere.

The Olympus camera has a lightweight, strong body which means it's easy to carry it anywhere

1 Geox shoes – breathable rubber soles allow your feet to breathe.
Geox shoes _____ breathable rubber soles _____ _____ _____ feet to breathe.

2 LG washing machine – an 11kg capacity in a standard-sized washer – you can wash more less often.
The LG washing machine _____ an 11kg capacity _____ _____ that you can wash more less often.

3 Deuter Speed Lite backpack – 100% airmesh* shoulder straps for optimum comfort.
The Deuter Speed Lite backpack _____ 100% airmesh shoulder straps _____ _____ optimum comfort.

4 Lego themed sets – a variety of fun themes for just about everyone.
Lego themed sets _____ a variety of fun themes _____ _____ _____ _____ _____ to find something for all children.

5 Braun shaver – adaptable head which fits to individual face contours for optimum shaving comfort.
The Braun shaver _____ an adaptable head _____ _____ _____ optimum shaving comfort.

6 Colgate toothpaste – 12 hours' anti-bacterial protection so you remain protected even between brushings.
Colgate toothpaste gives 12 hours' anti-bacterial protection _____ that you remain protected even between brushings.

*a strong lightweight material often used in outdoor equipment

3 Write the text (up to 150 words) for the homepage of a company which sells MP3 players. The aim of the text is to help the company boost their sales. The main features of the product are:

- 16GB memory
- Tough, hard-wearing case
- Stylish range of colours
- 50 hours' battery life

You can add other features which you think will help to sell the product.

11 Accounting

Vocabulary and Grammar

Key financial terms

1 Find four words which can go before 'costs' and put them in the spaces. The first letters have been given to help you.

1 d_____

2 i_____

3 v_____   (costs)

4 f_____

5 What is another word for number 2? o_____

2 Match the sentences below with the four different types from exercise 1. Each sentence can match with two types of costs. The first one has been done as an example.

1 Our raw materials costs have really gone up in the last month due to the rise in oil prices.

2 We've just renegotiated our lease and managed to keep the rent increase to only 3.5 percent.

3 We employ a lot of freelance staff who come in and help out in our busy periods.

4 Due to the type of products we make here, our insurance premiums are quite high.

5 Most of our permanent staff have worked here for more than five years.

A d_____ costs	B i_____ costs	C v_____ costs	D f_____ costs
1		1	

Different types of cost

1 Use the clues to find the words. The first letters have been given to help you.

1 Payment on a loan. i_____ (8 letters)

2 Keeping something in good condition. m_____ (11 letters)

3 A decline in value. d_____ (12 letters)

4 Plotting a course. n_____ (10 letters)

5 Provision of food and drink. c_____ (8 letters)

6 A guarantee of compensation. i_____ (9 letters)

2 Complete the text with the words from exercise 1.

If we want to make savings, we have to look at areas we can cut without affecting our customers. So, first, let's look at areas we can't cut. Obviously, as an airline, safety is and always will be our number one priority. We have a strict **1** _____ programme for all our planes to ensure they are always safe, and in excellent working condition. In addition, we have **2** _____ costs which provide protection should anything go wrong – we can't really make cuts there. We have to pay **3** _____ charges to enable us to fly over other countries' airspace. So, how about possible costs we can reduce? The loan we took out a few years ago to lease new aircraft has quite a high rate of **4** _____ , so we'll be speaking to the bank to see if we can reduce that. We can also offset the **5** _____ in value of our planes over time – generally things do decline slightly in value as time goes by. Finally, we could think about making cuts to the **6** _____ – do passengers really expect gourmet meals on flights? We could consider not serving hot food, but offering healthy snack food instead for short haul flights?

3 Match the two parts of the sentence to define three key types of costs.

1 Direct costs are	**a** costs for corporate and regional functions: **press office**.
2 Indirect costs are	**b** ones that can be identified with a particular project or activity: *catering*
3 Central costs are	**c** not directly accountable to a particular project or activity: *maintenance*

Now decide which type of cost is being referred to in each sentence. (1= direct cost, 2= indirect cost, 3= central cost). The first one has been done for you.

a The airport charges vary widely, depending on the country and the size of the airport. __1__

b We have interest payments of over €10,000 per year. _____

c Most of our staff are on permanent contracts. _____

d The value of our planes decreases each year. _____

e We usually lease the aircraft as this is more efficient than buying them. _____

f All the administration is done through our head office. _____

g Obviously, our fuel charges are directly related to oil prices. _____

h We try to keep our passenger handling costs as low as possible by offering self-service check-in. _____

Gerunds

1 Look at the following sentences and <u>underline</u> the gerund form.

1 We kept on buying from that supplier even after they closed the local office as we had a problem in sourcing a local firm.

2 I think we need to focus on keeping our costs down over the next quarter.

3 I'm afraid he doesn't seem interested in learning anything new even though we want to build up his experience of managing a larger group.

4 She's become very good at troubleshooting problems at an early stage as a result of spending time at the head office.

5 We all have to rise to the challenge of getting the most out of our staff in these difficult conditions.

2 Rearrange the words to form sentences using the gerund construction. The beginning and end of the sentences have been done for you.

1 As a result of _____ cost savings.
made introducing system significant new the we've

2 Unfortunately, _____ criticism.
very good not handling at he's

3 The company _____ staff.
in problems have retaining any doesn't

4 We need _____ to consumers.
on clear focus getting to a across message

5 If we can _____ on time.
rate at finish keep this we'll on easily working

3 Rewrite the sentences using the gerund form at the start.

1 It's easy to travel around the city by public transport.

_____

2 It's going to be a slow process to install the new computer system.

_____

3 The first stage in the process is to send out a questionnaire to all our customers.

_____

4 It's essential to find out everyone's requirements before we start.

_____

5 It's not very effective to study and work at the same time.

_____

4 Complete the sentences with the correct gerund form of the verb in brackets. You will also need to add a preposition.

1 We need to focus _____ _____ the new system as soon as possible. (integrate)

2 Our manager was quick to take up the challenge _____ _____ the first person to represent the company in the local marathon. (become)

3 We had very few problems _____ _____ qualified staff when we opened the new office in January. (recruit)

4 In our recent survey, a high percentage of people said they were interested _____ _____ 'green' products. (buy)

5 As a result _____ _____ the lower end of the market, we've increased our sales volume. (target)

Review!

41–42 Listen to tracks 41–42, which are from the Student's Book. Notice how the speakers use polite language and strategies to develop a good relationship with colleagues.

Polite language

1 **43** Listen to the following sentences 1–8 and match them with their function a–f.

1 I'm afraid I can't make the meeting on Friday. (*manager to staff*) _____

2 Would it be all right if I kept all the paperwork here? (*staff to manager*) _____

3 Gosh, you've done it so much more quickly than I could have. (*manager to staff*) _____

4 Oh, it was nothing, we only spent the whole weekend working on it! (*staff to staff*) _____

5 You've done a great job! Well done. (*manager to staff*) _____

6 Can I hold on to this a bit longer? Would that be OK? (*manager to manager*) _____

7 I'm really grateful for all your support. (*staff to manager*) _____

8 Sorry, James, I didn't realise you didn't want to be disturbed. (*manager to manager*) _____

a complimenting	**d** apologising
b offering praise	**e** requesting indirectly
c joking	**f** thanking

2 Look back at the sentences using polite language from exercise 1 and decide if they are type A (showing solidarity) or B (showing respect). Write the letter of your choice next to each number.

1 _____	**5** _____
2 _____	**6** _____
3 _____	**7** _____
4 _____	**8** _____

3 **44** Listen to part of a discussion about implementing a new accounting system and complete the gaps. Piotr and Tarja are managers and Jan and Tove are staff members.

Tarja: … OK, well, as you know we're about half-way through the changeover between the old accounting system and the new one and it seems to be going really well. I mean you two and the rest of the team **1** _____ _____ _____ _____ _____ _____ the project on track.

Piotr: Yes, can I just add that **2** _____ _____ _____ _____ _____ hard work, and

the fact that you've kept everyone on the team motivated has made a huge difference.

Jan: Oh, **3** _____ _____ _____ _____ , I mean all those weekends of overtime … !

Tarja: No, but seriously, you've done really well and **4** _____ _____ _____ _____ _____ _____ !

Tove: Well, it was pretty difficult at the beginning and **5** _____ _____ _____ _____ some of the early deadlines, but it seems to have settled down now.

Piotr: **6** _____ _____ _____ _____ _____ _____ _____ is where you think you need our support?

Tove: Well, we'll probably need …

Now match each of the six expressions above with the correct function (a–f).

a complimenting _____	**d** apologising _____
b offering praise _____	**e** requesting indirectly _____
c joking _____	**f** thanking _____

Vocabulary and Grammar

Word formations

1 Use the clues to find the words.

1 A person to whom money is paid. p_____ (5 letters)

2 Money that you have to pay for breaking an agreement.
p_____ (7 letters)

3 A promise that something will be done or will happen.
g_____ (9 letters)

4 Something which encourages someone to do something.
i_____ (9 letters)

5 To pay back. r_____ (5 letters)

6 Continuing over a long period of time. s_____ (11 letters)

7 To punish someone for breaking a rule or agreement.
p_____ (8 letters)

2 Complete the gaps by writing the correct form of the word in brackets at the end of the sentence.

1 The bank will probably _____ you for cutting short your loan. (penal)

2 The sales team are very demotivated at the moment, we need to think of a way to _____ them. (incentive)

3 The small loans that are given under microfinance schemes often have very high _____ rates – most borrowers pay the money back in full. (pay)

4 If you have a poor credit rating, it's often difficult to get a loan unless you have a personal _____ . (guarantee)

5 Grameen Bank is different from conventional banks because it does not charge a _____ if you do not pay the loan back on time. (penal)

6 The _____ of the loan will be the person responsible for ensuring it is paid back. (pay)

Strategies for understanding unknown words

1 Choose the best word for each gap from the choices below.

Microcredit is an important part of the growing microfinance sector, a movement which **1** _____ a world where low-income households have access to a wide range of financial services. Originally many microfinance institutions (MFIs) were **2** _____ set up by governments, but more and more credit institutions have microfinance departments in order to **3** _____ on this growing market. MFIs differ from traditional banks in several ways. Firstly, they do not always insist on **4** _____ to give a loan and secondly, there are often no **5** _____ if loans are not repaid on time. In addition, clients are often **6** _____ who may have difficulty maintaining steady cash-flow. Clients must be able to make regular **7** _____ and for this reason these loans are not suitable for the **8** _____ .

MFIs often operate in areas with a low population **9** _____ which can make administration costs higher. If MFIs are to operate **10** _____ , they need to be able to cover these costs with higher interest rates.

1 A believes	**B** envisions	**C** inspires
2 A companies	**B** committees	**C** entities
3 A profit	**B** capitalise	**C** incentivise
4 A collateral	**B** collaterals	**C** warrantees
5 A penalties	**B** rewards	**C** repayments
6 A house businesses	**B** homeworkers	**C** household based entrepreneurs
7 A pay	**B** repayments	**C** credits
8 A destitute	**B** subsistence	**C** substitute
9 A number	**B** density	**C** concentration
10 A reasonably	**B** healthily	**C** sustainably

2 In each sentence, there is one incorrect word. <u>Underline</u> the incorrect word and write the correct word at the end of the sentence.

1 Fines are being introduced to penalty people who do not disclose their earnings from investments. _____

2 The city is planning to capitalise in their recent success in the Tourism awards by building several new hotels. _____

3 The report claims that more than 20 percents of typical 'British' brands are owned by foreign entries. _____

4 The government has lifted the visa requires for visitors from a range of countries who were previously not allowed to enter without a visa. _____

5 It is a big responsibility to act as a guarantee for a loan – it means you are responsible if the loan is not paid back. _____

6 The company has just announced new packaging plans which they see as key to continuing to do business more sustainability in the future. _____

Used to, be used to and get used to

1 Look at the following sentences and decide if *used to* is an active or passive verb or an adjective.

Active verb _____   Adjective _____

Passive verb _____

1 That warehouse is being used to store surplus stock at the moment.
2 I'm not used to people taking phone calls in meetings.
3 We're going to have to get used to working more internationally.
4 They used to batch everything together in one shipment.
5 That machine is used to measure temperature.
6 We used to deal with much bigger orders.

2 Match the two halves of the sentences.

1 We used	a to having so much 'free' time, but he seems busier now than ever!
2 He's worked here a long time, so he's used	b to his management style yet.
3 The main assembly line is not being used	c to living on his own.
4 The sales department used	d to working a lot of overtime in the peak season.
5 Since he got divorced, he's gradually getting used	e to store some stationery at the moment.
6 The new boss is very hands-on and our team aren't used	f to manufacture those components but we stopped last year.
7 The conference room is being used	g to have a lot more autonomy before the restructuring.
8 After retiring, he thought he'd never get used	h to its full capacity at the moment.

3 Complete the following sentences with the correct form of the verbs in brackets.

1 I've only been in the UK for a couple of weeks, but I'm sure I _____ on the left soon! (drive)

2 Before the merger, we all _____ our own offices, but it's all open-plan now. (have)

3 It'll probably take a bit of time to _____ in the new team, but don't worry, I'm sure you'll fit in. (work)

4 I _____ the new software system a lot quicker than I expected. (use)

5 When I first started working here, I _____ the office layout really confusing, but now I _____ my way around. (find, find)

6 He's always lived close to the office, so he _____ long distances. (not commute).

7 I _____ breakfast meetings now, but when I first came here, it was a real shock. (have)

8 Although it seems difficult now, I'm sure we _____ with the new system by the time we go into full production. (work)

9 Since he got promoted, he _____ much earlier and finishing much later. (start)

10 We _____ all our components from one supplier, but we realised that was not a good strategy when they had some problems last year. (buy)

Skills

Review! 👁

45 Listen to track 45, which is from the Student's Book. Notice how Barack Obama stresses keywords, chunks language and controls the speed of his speech to give a clear and engaging presentation.

Use techniques to improve your delivery (stress, chunking and pace)

1 Look at the following sentences from a presentation about a new microfinance provider. Underline the stressed words and put a | between the words to show the pauses.

1 First of all I'd like to thank you all for coming today – it's great to see so many people.

2 So who are we and what do we do?

3 We aim to extend credit to some of the world's poorest people to help them to help themselves.

4 Unlike a traditional bank we will visit our customers – we don't expect them to come to us.

5 And there are no charges for late payments and no minimum loan amount.

6 That means anyone at any level can get credit from us.

46 Now listen to check your answers. Finally, listen and try to match the model.

2 Look at the following sentences from Barack Obama's speech, which have the wrong stress and pauses marked, and correct them.

This is | your victory. I know | you didn't | do this just to win | an election and I know | you didn't do it | for me. You | did it because | you understand the enormity | of the task that lies | ahead. For even | as we celebrate tonight, we | know the challenges | that tomorrow will | bring are the | greatest of our lifetime – two wars, a planet | in peril, the worst financial | crisis in a century.

47 Now listen to check your answers.

3 Now listen to part of Muhammad Yunus's presentation about Grameen Bank and complete the gaps.

The **1**_____ banks are based on one basic principle: the **2**_____ you have, the more you can get. We **3**_____ that principle. Our principle is this – the less you have, the more **4**_____ you are for us. In order to create a completely new bank, we have to get rid of the whole idea of **5**_____ . We said I don't need anything, I'll just give you a

6_____ . And that's what we do. We have no collateral. We have no **7**_____ .

48 Now, mark the stress and pauses. Finally, listen again and try to match the model.

CEF Can Do statements

Now you have completed the exercises in this unit, read the following statements. Tick the boxes that apply to you.

	Yes, I can do this.	I think I need more practice.
1 I can use key word formations connected with banking.	☐	☐
2 I can use grammatical structures with *used to, be used to* and *get used to*.	☐	☐
3 I understand and can use techniques to improve my presentation delivery.	☐	☐

If you need more practice on points 1–3, check your Student's Book:

1 Lesson 12.2   **2** Lesson 12.1   **3** Lesson 12.3

Make a note of the areas you need to practise more and how you can do this.

Microfinance sees demand leap

Small business owners in the UK are turning to microfinance, a system of credit more readily associated with helping people in developing countries escape poverty, as a result of the main UK retail banks continuing to refuse loan applications.

That is causing problems for microfinance providers. They typically lend much smaller amounts than these businesses require, and so need to spend more time conducting due diligence*. Those microfinance organisations that would like to expand to meet the demand then encounter problems of their own raising further finance to build their capital reserves.

Microfinance groups have in the past provided small sums of money to poor communities and to the self-employed, who have struggled to get reasonably priced loans or even banking services. The service has been hugely successful in Bangladesh, where Muhammad Yunus was awarded the Nobel Peace Prize for his achievements with his Grameen Bank.

However, microfinance is increasingly common in the west as a way to help people in deprived areas, often shunned by mainstream banks. Because of difficulty in obtaining loans and overdrafts from high street banks, microfinancers are targeted by businesses that would never have sought such help before.

Faisel Rahman, who founded Fair Finance to help some of the UK's most deprived communities in east London, said his organisation had been 'inundated*' by calls from conventional small businesses, many referred to his team by bank managers unable to lend money. Such interest places considerable pressure on organisations such as Fair Finance, which have their own capital constraints. 'The challenge for us is booming demand, good portfolios and little credit to lend,' Mr Rahman said.

Take Sky Garden, a green roofing business, that turned to the Fredericks Foundation, a charity to help the unemployed and ex-offenders* get back on their feet. It needed a £20,000 short-term loan to cover wages and other costs after cold weather had prevented the company from doing any work, and therefore bringing in money. Steve Raftery, Sky Garden's managing director, said: 'We were sitting on £500,000-worth of orders but the two months of downtime started causing problems.'

He was recommended to the Fredericks Foundation by a financial adviser after being turned down by several high street lenders. Mr Raftery had no trouble repaying the three-month £20,000 loan he eventually received from the foundation. The trouble was to persuade an organisation used to lending a few thousand pounds to give a five-figure sum to a single enterprise.

'The hoops we had to go through were significantly more demanding than any of the banks would have expected us to go through,' Mr Raftery said. For the Fredericks Foundation the situation was equally difficult. 'We did a lot more due diligence than usual because we could not afford to lose £20,000,' Paul Barry-Walsh, chairman, said. 'That was a large proportion of our loan capital for the year.'

---

*due diligence: the process of investigation by investors into the details of a potential investment.
* inundated: overwhelmed, having more demand than it was possible to deal with
*ex-offenders: people who have been in prison

Source: *Financial Times*, 12.09.10

1 Read the text and underline the correct option in each sentence.

1 Small businesses in the UK are starting to use microfinance because the *interest rate is good / they can't get credit from the banks*.

2 *Self-employed people / Medium-sized businesses* have typically used microfinance in the past.

3 Microfinance companies *don't want to lend capital to businesses / find it difficult to raise capital for larger loans*.

4 Sky Garden wanted to borrow money because *their business was unsuccessful / they had a cash-flow problem*.

5 Sky Garden had to go through a *complex / simple* process to get a loan.

6 The Fredericks Foundation spent a long time investigating Sky Garden because they *did not trust them to pay back the loan / do not normally lend such large amounts*.

2 Match the words from the text with the correct meaning.

1	leap (headline)	a	restrictions
2	encounter (paragraph 2)	b	period when a company is not earning
3	deprived (paragraph 4)	c	rise quickly
4	shunned (paragraph 4)	d	find, come across
5	constraints (paragraph 5)	e	refused to have contact with, ignored
6	downtime (paragraph 6)	f	extremely poor

3 Look at the last three paragraphs of the article and find expressions to match these definitions.

1 to become independent again after a difficult period

_____

2 holding / being in possession of _____

3 refused _____

4 a (difficult) process to follow _____

4 Without looking at the text, match the following words to make common expressions.

1	readily	a	finance
2	conduct	b	sum
3	meet	c	common
4	raise	d	associated
5	increasingly	e	areas
6	deprived	f	due diligence
7	five-figure	g	demand

Now check your answers with the text.

5 Complete the sentences with some of the expressions from exercises 2, 3 and 4.

1 Although microfinance is more _____ _____ with developing countries, many small businesses are using it after being _____ _____ by the bigger banks.

2 Many charities are set up to help _____ or less fortunate members of society _____ _____ _____ _____ _____ .

3 Microfinance organisations often _____ difficulties when lending larger sums as they have to _____ _____ _____ more thoroughly than the major banks.

4 It is becoming _____ _____ for companies to look at alternative ways to _____ _____ because banks are refusing credit.

5 Despite _____ _____ a large number of orders, companies may still have cash-flow problems if they have been unable to produce because of a period of _____ .

6 Microfinance organisations who want to _____ the growing _____ for credit sometimes find it difficult because of _____ on the amount they can lend.

7 It is unusual for a microfinance organisation to lend a _____ _____ to just one company.

Writing 6
Formal and informal emails at work

Formality and functions

1 Look at the following abbreviations and write down what each one stands for.

1 Cc = _____ _____

2 i.e. = _____ _____

3 re = _____

4 asap = _____ _____ _____
_____

5 BTW = _____ _____ _____

6 FYI = _____ _____ _____

7 PLS = _____

8 LOL = _____ _____ _____

2 Look at the abbreviations in exercise 1 and decide which can be used in formal or informal emails.

Some abbreviations may be used in both types of email.

Formal: _____   Informal: _____

Functions of emails

1 Look at the following sentences from emails 1–10 and match them with their functions a–g. Some can match with more than one function.

a informing	**e** confirming
b inviting	**f** apologising
c requesting	**g** developing a relationship
d thanking	

1 Thanks very much for your e-mail; it was good to meet you in August, and to hear about your research projects. _____

2 Just to say, I'll be around this afternoon if you want to discuss anything. _____

3 Sorry to have been slow getting back to you but there have been some delays in getting the contract finalised. _____

4 We are very much looking forward to meeting you on Friday with a view to developing a long-term relationship. _____

5 Herve – could you email the sales report to the marketing director and sales manager please? _____

6 The follow-up meeting will take place next Wednesday, 6 October, starting at 9.30 a.m.

7 Many thanks for getting back to me so quickly. _____

8 We'd very much like you to visit us in Dijon to see the factory here and to discuss different aspects of the project. _____

9 Could you check and get back to me as soon as possible? _____

10 If any of your sales representatives have new customers who need training on the new software, please let me know and we will get in touch. _____

2 Now, match sentences 1–10 from exercise 1, with situations a–c.

Example: a colleague to colleague, informal _____1____

a colleague to colleague, informal _____

b client to supplier / supplier to client, formal _____

c colleague to colleague, formal _____

3 **You work for a fruit juice manufacturer. You have received the following email from a potential client.**

```
Email                                                    [_][□][X]
To Address:  enquiries45@superjuice.co.uk            ▼
From Address: kristian.jansson23@healthdrinks.se     ▼
                                          [Save Mail...]

Hello
We are interested in distributing your products in the
Scandinavian market. Could you send us some more
information about your products and your pricing scale?
We would like to arrange a meeting with you next month
as we are visiting your area.
Regards
Kristian Jansson
```

Reply to the enquiry, giving the following information:

- You already have a distributor in Denmark, but nothing in the other Scandinavian countries.
- You are attaching information about pricing scales and a PDF of your brochure.
- You would be pleased to meet them in the 2nd or 4th weeks of next month if those dates are convenient.

Now write a short email to your boss, summarising the enquiry and your reply.

Vocabulary and Grammar

CSR topic vocabulary

1 Use the clues to find the words.

1 To be forced (to do something). c_____ (9 letters)

2 Not telling the whole truth. d_____ (9 letters)

3 Health and happiness. w_____ (9 letters)

4 Created. g_____ (9 letters)

5 Misleading somebody, for example you pretend to have knowledge that you do not have. b_____ (8 letters)

6 Very large. v_____ (4 letters)

2 Match the sentences 1–5 with the phrases they are referring to a–e.

1	It's important that I have enough time to spend with my family, I don't want to be working all the time.	**a**	stakeholders
2	I don't think they're really interested in our views, but they have to ask because it's part of the procedure.	**b**	primary purpose
3	We have a set of guidelines which regulate the way we buy goods and services.	**c**	work–life balance
4	We need to appeal to everyone who has an interest in our business, not just our suppliers and employees.	**d**	box-ticking exercise
5	The committee was set up last year with the main aim of improving inter-departmental communication.	**e**	procurement policies

3 Complete the text about CSR with the correct form of the words from exercises 1 and 2.

_____

CSR, many argue, is just a PR exercise: companies use it to improve their image in order to sell more and make **1** _____ profits. For some companies, this may well be the case: they believe the **2** _____ of business is to make money, and they do not want to be concerned with their impact on a wider range of **3** _____ outside the company. For such companies, the business world is a tough environment where **4** _____ is part of the 'game'. However, recent research has shown that, far from just being a **5** _____ , CSR policies which deal with ethical issues can actually boost revenues. Companies which are concerned about the **6** _____ of their employees, and ensure a good **7** _____ , find that employees are less stressed and more productive. Having **8** _____ which ensure that suppliers do not use child labour have a positive impact on the company image and help to avoid negative publicity. In fact, many of the top-rated FTSE companies have shown that implementing CSR policies has helped to **9** _____ increased revenues. These companies have demonstrated that they do not need to be **10** _____ to follow policies imposed from outside and that they do not need to **11** _____ customers or the public about their business practices. They have shown that 'doing the right thing' and making a profit are not contradictions in the business world.

_____

Phrases with prepositions

1 Complete the gaps with the correct prepositions.

1 Our latest advertising campaign, which was launched last month, generated a huge amount _____ interest.

2 The company should be increasingly mindful _____ its stakeholders in these difficult times.

3 The government's new strategy, which focuses _____ the poorest communities, has been welcomed at local level.

4 We have to be aware of the impact our decision will make _____ both our customers and suppliers.

5 These new brands will be incorporated _____ our existing portfolio of products and, we believe, will bring added value.

6 Following successful trials, the new policies will be integrated _____ our existing systems over the next few months.

7 The company needs to look _____ ways of increasing productivity without compromising quality.

8 The new regulations aim to make companies more transparent _____ the way they select and promote staff.

9 More and more people are becoming conscious _____ their impact on the environment and it's something our company image should reflect.

2 Sort the sentences in exercise 1 into the correct category, according to their structure.

a Verb + preposition + noun	b Noun + preposition + noun	c Adjective + preposition

3 In each sentence there is one incorrect word. <u>Underline</u> the incorrect word and write the correct word at the end of the sentence.

1 These principles are incorporated by our new mission statement which is available to view on our website. _____

2 Next year, the company want to focus on set up a new dealer network. _____

3 By choosing the more expensive option, we hope the impact to our customers will be minimal. _____

4 Due to the increased amount of working in the department, we have introduced some guidelines about overtime. _____

5 We're looking to taking over our rivals in order to gain a larger market share. _____

6 Our new mentoring system aims to help new employees feel integrated within the company much more quickly. _____

7 The team need to be mindful about their last match, when they were badly beaten by their closest rivals in the league. _____

8 The government is putting pressure on businesses in the financial sector to be more transparency in their M&A activities. _____

9 Some recent research has suggested that people may be too conscious on certain diseases and this can have an adverse effect on their health. _____

4 Choose the best word for each gap from the choices below.

So, let's 1 _____ our results for the year: our operating profit is up and we feel that's for a number of reasons. Firstly, we've focused much more 2 _____ to our customers and we've realised that in these difficult times they are more 3 _____ cost. So, we've 4 _____ some new, lower-priced, products into our range. Secondly, we're trying to be more 5 _____ the way we select our suppliers: we don't want people to think all the decisions are made in secret. In addition, we've 6 _____ a new set of selection criteria within our existing policy and this is sent out to all potential suppliers. Finally, we realised from the 7 _____ feedback we received that people were really concerned about our 8 _____ the environment, so we introduced our new refillable bottles which have been extremely successful. I think our results prove that being 9 _____ our responsibilities to both our customers and the wider community can be a very beneficial strategy.

1 **A** look to	**B** look at	**C** look for
2 **A** to listen	**B** to listening	**C** on listening
3 **A** concentrated on	**B** conscious of	**C** thinking about
4 **A** integrated	**B** incorporated	**C** initiated
5 **A** transparency in	**B** transient about	**C** transparent in
6 **A** incorporated	**B** introduced	**C** involved
7 **A** capacity of	**B** volume in	**C** amount of
8 **A** impression of	**B** impact on	**C** image of
9 **A** aware to	**B** mindful of	**C** conscious about

Skills

Review! 🎧

🎧 **49–51** Listen to tracks 49–51, which are from the Student's Book. Notice how the speakers open the conversations, use specific words to actively listen and respond and also use the correct level of formality.

Supporting the speaker through listener responses

1 🎧 **52** Listen to the following mini-dialogues and complete the gaps. If nothing is said, write 'silence' in the gap.

1 A: I'm not totally happy with the next one.

B: _____ _____ .

2 A: But, you're not actually directly giving money back to the community as such.

B: _____ , _____ .

3 A: Well I'll change that to 'support' if 'sponsorship' is too strong a word. So that's fine.

B: _____ . _____ . _____ .

4 A: It's not exactly what I had in mind.

B: _____ .

5 A: So, you think we can get it done by Friday, yeah?

B: _____ .

6 A: I think it'll look great, don't you?

B: _____ .

7 A: I'll try and send that off to you a bit later.

B: _____ .

8 A: I think the team are starting to work really well together.

B: _____ , _____ .

2 Now listen to the dialogues again and decide if the responses in exercise 1 are positive, negative or neutral.

Positive: _____

Negative: _____

Neutral: _____

3 🎧 **53** Listen to the following dialogue between two colleagues on the phone and mark the intonation on numbers 1, 2, 4 and 5.

Ken: Hi, Sarah. Ken here.

Sarah: Hi, Ken. Good to hear from you. Everything OK?

Ken: Yes, very good. Just calling about sorting out the brochure.

Sarah: **1** <u>Oh.</u>

Ken: It's just that it's not finished at the moment.

Sarah: **2** <u>Hmm.</u>

Ken: But, we also need to try and get down on paper what our mission is as clearly as possible.

Sarah: **3** _____

Ken: Do you agree?

Sarah: **4** <u>Maybe.</u> What do you suggest we change?

Ken: Well, there are three headings there. The first one is leadership, then communication and then sustainable tourism, yes?

Sarah: **5** <u>Uh-huh.</u>

Now make the conversation more supportive by choosing the best option a–c to replace the existing responses 1–5.

1 a Maybe.
(rising intonation)
b Sure.
(flat intonation)
c Great.
(rising intonation)

2 a silence
b Uh-huh.
(rising intonation)
c Oh.
(flat intonation)

3 a Sure.
(falling intonation)
b Sure.
(rising intonation)
c Uh-huh.
(flat intonation)

4 a Absolutely.
(rising intonation)
b Hmm.
(flat intonation)
c Sure.
(flat intonation)

5 a Maybe.
(flat intonation)
b Absolutely.
(falling intonation)
c Sure.
(rising intonation)

CEF Can Do statements

Now you have completed the exercises in this unit, read the following statements. Tick the boxes that apply to you.

	Yes, I can do this.	I think I need more practice.
1 I can use key vocabulary connected to CSR.	☐	☐
2 I can use phrases accurately with the correct dependent preposition.	☐	☐
3 I am more aware of how to be an active, supportive listener and how this helps to improve conversations.	☐	☐

If you need more practice on points 1–3, check your Student's Book:

1 Lesson 13.1   **2** Lesson 13.2   **3** Lesson 13.3

Make a note of the areas you want to practise more and how you can do this.

14 Strategic planning

Vocabulary

Verbs for strategic planning

1 Look at the following sentences and replace the <u>underlined</u> words and phrases with a verb with a similar meaning. You may need to change the form of the verb.

1 We'll be <u>carrying out</u> a survey of all our users in the next two months. _____
2 I decided to <u>go to</u> my manager about the problem with the product. _____
3 We'll probably <u>put</u> this plan <u>into action</u> at the beginning of next year when all the staff have returned from holiday. _____
4 Unfortunately, we didn't <u>clearly identify</u> whether we wanted the electric or battery-operated model and so they've sent us the wrong one. _____
5 We routinely <u>check, observe and record</u> students throughout the course and this contributes to their final result. _____
6 We were advised not to <u>change direction</u> from the agreed route as some areas of the city were dangerous. _____
7 <u>Making sure</u> customers are satisfied is our number one priority.

2 In each sentence, there is one incorrect word. <u>Underline</u> the incorrect word and write the correct word at the end of the sentence.

1 Now we've decided on the new procedures, we need to specify them, but I suggest we wait until a quieter time. _____
2 We need to develop the property at all times because of the recent thefts. _____
3 This room has enough space for us to consult the meeting. There is a large table, chairs and also a screen for computer presentations. _____
4 To implement a brand-new product from the ideas stage to the market and selling stage we are going to need 30 million Euros. _____
5 Let's not conduct from the main point of the meeting, we need to discuss the new brochure now. _____
6 We are offering staff a bonus to implement they come to the training sessions for the new software program. _____
7 I need to ensure the company accountant before we make a decision about this contract with the new supplier. _____

3 An HR manager is explaining his company's change in recruitment strategy. Choose the best word for each gap from the choices below.

As you may know, last year we decided to **1** _____ a major review of our hiring policy. We felt we needed to **2** _____ a new strategy to address the problems we've identified with the age profile of our employees. Basically, we realised that due to the cuts we made in our graduate programme, we had **3** _____ from our earlier policy of keeping a good mixture of ages amongst our employees. So, the first thing we did was to **4** _____ everyone involved: we wanted to hear people's opinions and experiences. We then discussed the feedback with an external consultant and **5** _____ several options for a new strategy. One thing we **6** _____ very clearly was that we didn't want to change the age profile so drastically that existing staff felt uncomfortable. We're now in the process of **7** _____ the new system and we appreciate your patience with the changes it involves. During the coming months we'll be **8** _____ the new process to **9** _____ that we're achieving our goal of creating a good balance of ages and experience within our company.

1 **A** conduct	**B** consult	**C** evaluate
2 **A** conduct	**B** specify	**C** develop
3 **A** deviated	**B** developed	**C** implemented
4 **A** evaluate	**B** consult	**C** develop
5 **A** evaluated	**B** monitored	**C** consulted
6 **A** consulted	**B** ensured	**C** specified
7 **A** ensuring	**B** specifying	**C** implementing
8 **A** implementing	**B** monitoring	**C** conducting
9 **A** specify	**B** ensure	**C** consult

Multi-word verbs and collocations

1 **Find the correct preposition to complete the multi-word verb which matches the definition.**

get   **1** _____ _____   have a good rapport with

     2 _____   recover (after an illness or difficult period)

     3 _____ _____   do something successfully although it is not the best way of doing it.

come **4** _____ _____   encounter a difficult problem

     5 _____   find, discover unintentionally

     6 _____   be approved, gain approval

put   **7** _____   postpone, change to a later date

     8 _____ _____   tolerate

     9 _____   communicate, explain

take **10** _____   hire (staff)

    11 _____   start, resume (a hobby, sport)

    12 _____   buy, acquire (a company)

2 **Match the two halves of the sentences.**

1 He's been offered the job, but he's taking his time	**a** forward in the right direction.
2 His experience as a store manager held him	**b** with some new ideas for improving our service.
3 The purpose of this meeting is to come up	**c** over the decision as he doesn't want to make the wrong choice.
4 The company set	**d** to where it is today is the determination of the founder.
5 We try to get our philosophy	**e** in good stead when he decided to apply for a senior management position.
6 I think it's been a very productive discussion and we're certainly moving	**f** up the new office in Shanghai just two years ago and it's already our most successful operation.
7 We've had some great ideas generated today so the next step is to put	**g** across to the customer at every opportunity.
8 I think the main reason the company got	**h** some of them into practice.

3 **Choose the best word to complete the gaps.**

1 We'd like to take _____ your offer of free delivery. (on / up / off).

2 I think he tried to get _____ inventing some information on his CV because he was worried he didn't have the experience for the job. (away with / away / through)

3 While I was doing some research the other day, I came _____ some information which I thought would be useful for you. (through / up / across)

4 You have to put _____ protective clothing to enter the factory. (up / on / into)

5 My transfer approval finally came _____ last week, so I'll be moving next month. (off / up / through)

6 The company suffered badly in the last recession, but we're getting _____ it now, as the economy is beginning to improve. (on with / over / across)

7 After the last advertising campaign, sales really took _____ : the product was a great success. (off / over / up).

8 Due to the rising costs of raw materials, we'll have to put _____ our prices. (down / up / up with)

9 Unfortunately, we've come _____ some difficulties which have slowed the whole process down. (up with / against / up against)

10 The atmosphere in the department has been very uncomfortable recently – I think it's because the director and the new recruit don't get _____ (on with / over / on).

Review! 🔍

🎧 54–56 **Listen to tracks 54–56, which are from the Student's Book. Notice how the speakers tell their stories using narrative tenses and expressions.**

Narrative tenses

1 🎧 57 **Listen to this short narrative and complete the gaps.**

'Of course, when you work in the retail business, you often have funny experiences with customers, but one that I'll always remember was in my first job. I **1** _____ _____ as a shop assistant in a very expensive boutique in Milan. It was a Monday and the shop was actually closed, but I **2** _____ _____ in to do some stock-taking. While I **3** _____ _____ the stock, there was a loud knock. So, I **4** _____ up to the door and who should be standing there but a very famous football player and his girlfriend! As I **5** _____ only _____ in the job a short time, I **6** _____ _____ open the shop on my own, so I **7** _____ my boss. My boss was so shocked at first she couldn't say anything, but then she just **8** _____ 'Open the door, open the door!' So, we ended up opening the shop just for the footballer and his girlfriend, but it was worth it!'

Now, sort the verbs into the following categories.

Past simple: _____   Past continuous: _____

Past perfect: _____   Historic present: _____

Answering questions in interviews

1 🎧 64 **Listen to three short clips of anecdotes and match them to the following interview questions.**

a Can you tell me about a difficult experience you had, and how you reacted?
b How would your friends describe you?
c What do you think is your greatest achievement in your life?

1 _____   2 _____   3 _____

2 **Now, listen again to the anecdotes and complete the gaps.**

1 Yes, when I first started my present job, all the staff _____ _____ _____ everything by hand – there were no computers, even for the most basic information tasks. I think the staff really wanted to change, but the managing directsor, who was also the owner, _____ _____ the point … So, eventually I was able to go to the manager with all the

information and persuade him to invest in computers and so I feel that was a really good achievement.

2 I think, if I want something, nothing will stop me – I mean, for example, we _____ _____ a team-building event the other week and we had to complete this outside course, but I _____ _____ my trainers … anyway, I _____ some trainers just by the door – obviously someone's taken them off to come in, so I just take those and carry on … so, my friends might say I was a bit ruthless, but I think I'm competitive.

3 When my company was taken over last year, I had a new boss, and he insisted that we were all on call all the time. Well, our team _____ _____ _____ like that before and didn't really see why we should change … in the end, we called a meeting and _____ a rota so that only one of us was on call out of hours and that seems to have solved the problem.

CEF Can Do statements

Now you have completed the exercises in this unit, read the following statements. Tick the boxes that apply to you.

	Yes, I can do this.	I think I need more practice.
1 I can use the appropriate verbs to discuss / talk about strategic planning.	☐	☐
2 I am able to use multi-word verbs and expressions to talk about company strategy.	☐	☐
3 I can use narrative structures to tell a story or anecdote in an interview.	☐	☐

If you need more practice on points 1–3, check your Student's Book:

1 Lesson 14.1   2 Lesson 14.2   3 Lesson 14.3

Make a note of the areas you want to practise more and how you can do this.

Reading 7
Henry Mintzberg

Henry Mintzberg: Strategy Guru

Background
Professor Henry Mintzberg (born September 2, 1939) is an internationally renowned academic and author on business and strategic management. He is currently the Cleghorn Professor of Management Studies at McGill University in Montreal, Canada. He has been teaching there since 1968, after earning his Master's degree in Management (M.B.A.) and Ph.D. from the MIT Sloan School of Management in 1965 and 1968 respectively.

Key Thinking
Henry Mintzberg writes prolifically on the topics of management and business strategy, with more than 140 articles and thirteen books to his name. His most important book, The Rise and Fall of Strategic Planning, criticises some of the practices of strategic planning today and is considered required reading for anyone who seriously wants to take on a strategy-making role within their organisation. Tom Peters, American business guru and writer, named this as his favourite book of the past 25 years, 'no contest'.

He recently published a book entitled Managers Not MBAs which outlines what he believes to be wrong with management education today. Rather controversially, he singles out prestigious graduate management schools like Harvard Business School and the Wharton Business School at the University of Pennsylvania as examples of how obsession with numbers and an over-zealous attempt at making management into a science can actually damage the discipline of management. He also suggests that a new masters program, targeted at practising managers (as opposed to younger students with little real world experience), and emphasising practical issues, may be more suitable.

Ironically, although Professor Mintzberg is quite critical about the strategy consulting business, he has twice won the McKinsey Award for publishing the best article in the Harvard Business Review.

Contribution
Henry Mintzberg is one of the most interesting of management thinkers. He has made a major contribution to the study of strategy as a craft, the roles of managers, and management education. He has deliberately avoided the guru seminar trail and forged a unique intellectual path.

His approach to the areas he has researched has been similar. He is never content to accept what he is told or follow the established line. He prefers to take the mechanism apart to see for himself how it works. His characteristic approach is shown when he examines what managers really do, instead of accepting what they say they do or telling them what they ought to do. The same is true when he investigates the field of strategy, the area where he carried out perhaps his most influential work.

Recent Achievements
Mintzberg has won honours for his work from prominent practitioners and academic management communities: in the year 2000 he received the Distinguished Scholar Award from the Academy of Management, which brings together management academics from around the world. Named as an officer of the Order of Canada, he has also received thirteen honorary degrees from universities around the world.

Mintzberg has spent much of the past ten years with colleagues from five countries establishing a new generation of programs for management and organisation development, all rather novel ways to help managers learn from their own experience.

Dr. Henry Mintzberg spends his public life dealing with organisations and his private life escaping from them.

Source: *Easy-strategy.com, by* Osama El-Kadi

1 **Read the article and match the events with the correct time.**

1	1939	**a**	starts teaching at McGill University
2	1965	**b**	receives Distinguished Scholar Award
3	1968	**c**	establishing new programs for management
4	1968	**d**	born
5	2000	**e**	gains Master's degree
6	last 10 years	**f**	Cleghorn Professor of Management Studies
7	today	**g**	gains PhD

2 **Read the article again. Are the statements true (T) or false (F)?**

1 *The Rise and Fall of Strategic Planning* is not critical of some ways of strategic planning. _____

2 *Managers not MBAs* suggests a more practical, less scientific approach to training managers. _____

3 Even though Mintzberg has criticised the consulting business, he has won awards for his articles. _____

4 Mintzberg is happy to accept what managers say they do. _____

5 Mintzberg's latest project is developing new management theory programs. _____

6 Mintzberg likes to spend his free time helping organisations. _____

3 **Look at the following sentence from paragraph 5 of the text and decide which sentence best summarises it.**

He has deliberately avoided the guru seminar trail and forged a unique intellectual path.

a He wants to be different from other gurus so he doesn't give seminars.

b He thinks differently and has followed a different direction from many other gurus.

4 **Find words or phrases in the text to match the following definitions.**

1 famous (paragraph 1) _____

2 extensively, a large amount (paragraph 2) _____

3 greatly respected (of a place) (paragraph 3) _____

4 too enthusiastic or eager (paragraph 3) _____

5 having a great effect on (paragraph 6) _____

6 important, well-known (paragraph 7) _____

7 unique, unusual (paragraph 8) _____

5 **Without looking at the text, match the following words to make common expressions.**

1	earn	**a**	out
2	take on	**b**	a role
3	single	**c**	a contribution
4	take apart	**d**	a degree
5	make	**e**	a mechanism

Now look back at the text to check your answers. Which of the above phrases are defined below?

a to dis-assemble or break down a large machine into smaller pieces or components _____

b to pick out one person or thing from a larger group _____

6 **Complete the sentences using the expressions from exercises 4 and 5. You may need to change the form of some of the verbs.**

1 Our company is internationally _____ for making these products – in fact, we have won several _____ awards for their design and manufacture.

2 After _____ my degree from the London School of Economics, I read a number of Charles Handy's books which were very _____ on my choice of career.

3 Although Mintzberg's ideas are sometimes _____ or unique, he has clearly _____ a valuable _____ to management thinking.

4 After I joined the company, I was _____ _____ for the fast-track management programme. Following that, I _____ _____ the role of assistant marketing director.

5 Unfortunately, one of the maintenance engineers was a little _____ and he _____ _____ the whole machine, rather than just replacing one or two parts.

Writing 7
First contact emails

Analysing emails

1 Look at the following excerpts from emails 1–4 and match them to their function a–c.

1 … I'm afraid to say that there have been some difficulties with the order. We didn't expect to receive 50 units of a 100-unit order 3 weeks after the first 50 units were delivered …

2 … Having worked in the industry for 10 years, I have developed a wide range of skills that would meet the expectations for the role. I am responsible for 35 staff, forming a cohesive team which helps the company meet its overall objectives.

3 … Jan's asked for all the figures as he's giving a big presentation to the Board – could you possibly send them to him?

4 … We manufacture furniture and have seen your products at trade fairs. We would be interested to know more about these products and if you were able to supply in large quantities …

a request _____ **b** complaint _____ **c** job application _____

Now decide if each is formal (F) or informal (I).

1 _____ 2 _____ 3 _____ 4 _____

What is the tone of each email? Choose one word from a, b and c.

1 a respectful / friendly; **b** convergent / divergent; **c** direct / indirect

_____

2 a respectful / friendly; **b** convergent / divergent; **c** direct / indirect

_____

3 a respectful / friendly; **b** convergent / divergent; **c** direct / indirect

_____

4 a respectful / friendly; **b** convergent / divergent; **c** direct / indirect

_____

Tone through word choice

1 Look at the following sentences and decide if they are formal (F) or informal (I).

1 I'd like to express my gratitude for the support you've provided throughout the project. _____

2 After just a few months, we've obtained an impressive level of repeat business. _____

3 It looks like we've had a bad month for sales. _____

4 We really need to talk about this as soon as possible. _____

2 Match the sentences with phrasal verbs 1–6 with their more formal equivalents a–f.

1 I can't figure out what went wrong.

2 Could you pass this on to all the relevant people?

3 Can we get back to the main point here, please?

4 No one's put forward any realistic suggestions.

5 Demand for this model is going down and there's no replacement.

6 The new owners are thinking of breaking up the existing department into several new, smaller teams.

a I think we need to return to the main item on the agenda.

b We are considering separating the department into several smaller teams.

c I'm afraid no one has proposed anything we can go ahead with at present.

d The demand for this model is decreasing and we haven't got a replacement.

e I don't understand what happened.

f I'd appreciate it if you could communicate this to everyone involved.

3 Look at the following sentences from an email requesting feedback. Put them in the correct order.

1 I've prepared some initial thoughts on this in the attached document. _____

2 Please let me have your feedback by the end of next week. _____

3 First, my thanks to you all for your help with the pilot scheme this year. _____

4 This reviews what we have done this year and gives my views on what this experience suggests for a larger and more systematic scheme. _____

5 Many thanks for your help and I look forward to hearing from you. _____

6 I will then collate all the information in one document and circulate it to you the following week. _____

4 Choose one of the following situations and write an email of about a 100 words. Remember to think about the style, tone and formality of your writing.

a a job application for a job you are interested in / would like to do

b a formal request for information from someone you do not know

c an informal request for information from a colleague or friend

Wordlist

1 Competitive environment

acted illegally

business environment

heavily regulated

impressive and symbolic order

increasingly globalised

invested heavily

largely monopolised

legal and technical monopoly

monopoly

natural monopoly

oligopoly

perfect competition

political and economic agenda

sustainable and profitable growth

2 Future uncertainty

conversely

genetically modified

massive

organic

purchase

reconsidering

shape

shortages

FMCG (fast-moving consumer goods)

consumer electronics

food and drink

health and beauty

home care

home electrical

supermarket retail

STEEP analysis

Socio-cultural

Technological

Economic

Environmental

Political

3 Rewarding performance

annual base salary

comparison companies

compensation programme

customer retention rates

difficult to incentivise

equity-based awards

financial incentive

incentive bonus

incentivise investment in

income

increased shareholder value

new product revenue

operating cash flow

operating profit

pay

pay cut

payment

performance-related pay

remuneration

reward

salary

short-term cash incentives

stretch goals / stretch targets

wage

4 Fostering creativity

convergence

creativity

divergence

imagination

implementation

innovation

interaction

invention

5 Organisational cultures

atmosphere at work

budgets

departments

dress code

expense accounts

norms

organisational structures

personality

procedures

reward systems

role culture

rules

task culture

values

6 Working across cultures

competence

dignity

face

identity

rapport

social inclusion

sociality rights

Nouns to make positive and negative judgments

create/seek synergy/synergies between/among/with

seize/explore/exploit (an) opportunity/opportunities for/to

give/stand/create/have/get (a) chance/chances to/of

raise/resolve/avoid conflict/conflicts between/of (especially conflict(s) of interests)

solve/cause/have (a) problem/problems with

inhibit/lack/enhance transparency/transparencies in/between

7 Change management

at the coalface

crave the limelight

gut-wrenching

peter out

run into trouble

tackle the thorny issues

take root

windows of opportunity

8 Project management

brief overview

cut costs

encourage teamwork

engaging the stakeholders

gather information

increase confidence

initial

pilot (the solution)

put (a plan) into practice

requirements

screen out unwanted projects

slash delivery times

undertake (a feasibility study)

9 E-marketing

4Cs

4Ps

bricks and clicks operator

bricks retailer

communication with the customer

convenience to the customer

cost to the customer

customer relationship marketing

customer wants and needs

customer's perspective

database marketing

dot.com

e-retail shop

e-tailer

marketing mix

multi-channel retailer

physical store

producer's perspective

pure play

retail outlet

search engine optimisation

social media marketing

target consumers

virtual store

web optimisation

10 Branding

asset

attributed to

beyond

boost

brand awareness

brand equity

brand extension

brand image

brand positioning

brand repositioning

extensions

gross revenues

licensed brand

luxury brand

manufacturer's brand

own brand

perceptions

transmit

Describing brands and products

affordable – style brand footwear

iconic – brand footwear look

inspirational – feel colours combinations

physical – pleasure comfort brand

relaxed – style feel look

to be inspired by

uncomplicated – style look

unmistakable features

versatile – combinations features footwear

vibrant – spirit colours style

11 Accounting

catering

central costs

depreciation

direct costs

fixed costs

indirect costs

insurance

interest

maintenance

navigation

overheads

variable costs

12 Microfinance

capitalise on

collateral

entities

envisions

guarantor

household-based entrepreneurs

incentive

incentivise

payee

payment

penalty

population density

repayment

requirement

sustainably

the destitute

to guarantee

to pay

to pay back

to penalise

to repay

13 Corporate social responsibility

amount of interest

bluffing

box-ticking exercise

compelled

conscious of

deception

focus on the impact

generated

impact on

incorporated within the strategy

integrated into the company

look at

mindful of

primary purpose

procurement policies

stakeholders

transparent in

vast

well-being

work–life balance

14 Strategic planning

conduct

consult

develop

deviate

ensure

evaluate

implement

monitor

specify

Multi-word verbs

come across

come on

come over

come through

come up against

come up with

get away

get away with

get on

get on with

get over

get up

move forward in the right direction

put across

put away

put down

put ideas into practice

put into

put off

put on

put up

put up with

take away

take in

take off

take on

take out

take over

take time over a decision

take up

Phrase Bank

Discourse Markers (Unit 2)

I mean we need to think about how it will impact on our sales …

It's more a question of what will, happen if we don't upgrade …

Obviously this creates a business risk for us because …

OK, we may as well start.

Right, the next thing we need to discuss is prices …

So, how do we start? Well, I've already done this.

So, just to give you a bit of background. Mainstream support for the present system expired …

We need to get through this and *then* we can finish …

We've worked with that supplier for years. *On the other hand*, we know we can get the components more cheaply elsewhere …

Well, I think *it's time to* start …

Vague Language (Unit 3)

I think we need to discuss salaries *and things like that* …

I want to have a proper exit strategy where other people are in place *and that kind of thing.*

It will probably cost about $40 a unit.

It's difficult having to work through lunch *and all that kind of thing* …

It's not a huge issue but it may become one one day …

There were people there who were certainly paid *probably more than double* what I'm being paid …

We *might* be able to do it …

Which means I'm pretty much solely responsible for keeping projects on track and budgets *and everything else* …

Checking/clarifying vague language (Unit 3)

By 'all that stuff' you mean …

How sure of that are you?

So by 'other things' you mean …

So you mean …

So you mean … is that right?

Evaluative metaphors and idioms (Unit 4)

(That's) a good way forward …

(the plans were) completely unreal …

(the rent is) stupid …

(These are) solid plans …

a pair of the right hands

a serious cost on top

find the problem out

getting a balance

have an issue with

high level of cover

I would really welcome that.

It eats into the time …

It's down to you to …

looking good …

sticks in the throat

That's absolute madness …

there's just a way around it

troubleshoot (the problem)

twenty-four/seven

Strategically summarising a position (Unit 5)

All I'm saying is that the attitude has got to slightly change.

My point is there's going to have to be a mindset change.

So this means that they can come across like this as they only focus on the technical …

What I mean is the technical people don't feel as if they're really part of this process …

What we're talking about is improving the attitude of the technical team.

Clarifying what you mean (Unit 5)

Having discussed it with them, *it's mostly about* ownership, I think …

I just think it's one of those things where they'll find lots of excuses not to do it.

I'm just saying that when you do get a change like this it's very important that everybody changes with it.

I'm not saying that. I think they're fabulous with customers. *What I'm saying is* that if the customer …

If this is going to happen *I think, to be honest with you*, their attitude's got to be 'customer' …

They've got to be very customer facing and their attitude has got to change, *which is what I just said.*

Metaphors of Movement (Unit 6)

Can we move on?

I *haven't got anywhere* with them.

I'm completely lost, I'm afraid.

It felt like we were *going backwards* at one point.

It was obvious that things were *going nowhere* at one particular stage.

So things are *moving forward* from that side of things.

The first step is to decide on our new prices … *the next step* is to contact all our customers …

Cohesion and referencing (Unit 7)

If you read the word *thus*, then it will be followed by a consequence relating to the information mentioned previously.

If you read the phrase *that sounds reasonable, but*, then you would expect to read something unusual that contrasts with the information mentioned before.

If you read the words *those actions*, then you know the actions were mentioned before.

If you read the words *they assume*, then you know that named people's opinions were stated previously.

If you read the words *two different groups of people*, then the information will follow that names and contrasts these two groups.

If a sentence or clause starts with *however*, then the information that follows will contrast with the information mentioned before.

Introducing and linking slides (Unit 10)

… and we focus specifically on …

Hi, my name is … and I'm …

If you're interested in pursuing this conversation, we look forward …

Moving on now to …

Now, I'd like to talk about …

Now let's look at …

Now let's turn to …

Over the next 5 minutes I'll give you a brief introduction of …

So how can we help …?

So what are the main challenges facing HQs …?

The way we start our work is to focus first on …

We're an e-marketing agency based in …

Well, we've seen a big change in the role a headquarters had over …

Using 'if' to persuade and direct staff (Unit 10)

If I'm opening car doors at the front door, I say 'Welcome.'

If you see a customer, you always smile at him or her.

Grammar reference

Unit 1: Tenses that talk about the past

Simple past

We use the simple past to talk about single events, habitual events or states which happened in the past. When we use this form, we are indicating that the event is 'finished'.

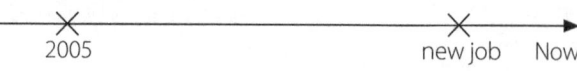

Example: I *graduated* in 2005. I *started* my new job last year.

Other common time phrases with the simple past are:

- ago
- yesterday

Example: I *worked* for IBM 15 years ago.

Past continuous

We use the past continuous to talk about events in progress around a particular time in the past or which are a background to other events which interrupt them.

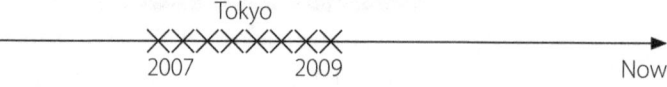

Example: I *was living* in Tokyo from 2007 to 2009.

Other common time phrases with the past continuous are:

- while
- as

Example: I passed the new stadium as I was coming home last night.

Past perfect

We use the past perfect to describe an event which happened before another past event.

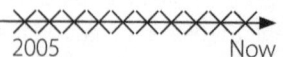

Example: We *had* already carried out the tests when we launched the new product.

Other common time phrases with past perfect are:

- by
- before

Example: I had never heard him speak before we went to the conference last year.

Present perfect

We use the present perfect to talk about events in the past which have a connection to the present. When we use this form, we are indicating that the time is 'unfinished' and the event affects the present.

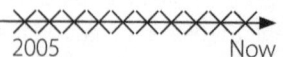

Example: I've *worked* for my company since 2005. (I still work for the company now)

Example: We've *lost* the contract, so we don't need that equipment any more. (past action, present result)

Example: I've just seen the CEO outside the building. (recent past)

Example: I've *visited* Singapore several times. (time not known or not stated)

Other common time phrases with present perfect are:

- already
  Example: We've already completed the project.

- yet
  Example: Have you heard about the new job yet?

- this (week/year/month etc.)
  Example: The company hasn't made a profit this year.

- so far
  Example: All the deliveries have been on time so far.

- this is the (first/second etc.) time
  Example: This is the first time we've worked with Canadians.

Unit 2: Future certainty and uncertainty

When we are giving our *opinions* about the future (rather than talking about our *plans*), we often use *modal verbs*. We also often introduce our opinions using verbs such as *think, suppose, guess* or adverbs such as *definitely, possibly, probably, perhaps, (un)likely*. These tell the listener or reader how certain we are.

Expressing certainty

Example: I think the company must / is going to — will definitely launch a new range next year.

Expressing probability

Example: I think the situation — is (highly) likely to / might well / may well / will probably — get worse.

I think it's (highly) unlikely that we'll get a pay rise this year.

Expressing possibility

Example: I think/guess*/suppose* we — may / might — possibly withdraw the product. — could

*These verbs often express quite a low level of possibility: the speaker is unsure.

Unit 3: Compound nouns

Compound nouns are formed by putting nouns (and adjectives) together. There are several common patterns:

adjective + noun, noun + noun and adjective + adjective or noun + noun

adjective + noun

Example: operating profit

The adjective describes the noun.

noun + noun

Example: compensation programme

The first noun acts like an adjective and describes the second noun.

adjective + adjective or noun + noun

Example: annual base salary, new product revenue

The adjective and the first noun both describe the second noun.

Using compound nouns

In English, using compound nouns sounds more natural than using an expression with *of*. For example, using *comparison companies* sounds better than *companies **of** comparison*. However, there are some fixed expressions where *of* is necessary:

Example: freedom of information, lack of choice

Compound nouns are very common in business English, particularly in writing.

Common adjectives with *sales* in writing are:

deferred, lengthy, direct, short, retail, worldwide, preapproved

However, when they are used in speaking, often different combinations are used:

Example: pre-, post-, unit, web, many

There are also compound nouns made up of <u>noun + noun + noun</u>, e.g. *customer retention rates*, and in these cases, the first two nouns act as adjectives. In order to understand the meaning of these types of compound noun, it is easier to start with the last noun: so, *customer retention rates* means the rate of retention of customers.

Some compound nouns are written as one word.

Example: output blackberry undercut software highlight

Unit 4: Past modals

In English, past modals are formed like this:

modal verb (e.g. *must*) + *have* + past participle (e.g. *given, started*)

We use past modals to talk about past events.

We use *might* + have + past participle if the speaker is not completely sure about the event. This form can be used to suggest different outcomes.

Example: I haven't seen him recently – he might have gone on holiday.

We use *could* + *have* + past participle if it is a past *possibility* which *did not come true*. This form can be used to suggest different outcomes or to express regret.

Example: We could have got the contract, but we didn't submit the tender in time.

We use *should(n't)* + have + past participle if it is something which was(n't) *advisable* in the past. This form is often used to *criticise* past decisions.

Example: It was a very successful product – they shouldn't have changed the design.

Example: It was a very good remuneration package – she should've accepted it.

We use *must* + *have* + past participle if the speaker is *sure* that this is the result of something that happened. This form can be used to make a *deduction* about past events.

Example: He wasn't on the train – he must have decided to drive.

We use *can't* + *have* + past participle if the speaker is *sure* this did *not* happen. This form can be used to make a *deduction* about past events.

Example: He can't have read the memo about parking, otherwise he wouldn't have come by car.

Unit 5: Question forms

Questions in English have two main purposes: to get a response and to comment on what someone has said.

'Response' questions

The typical structure for 'response' questions is:

Question word	auxiliary or modal	subject	main verb
Why	don't	we	meet at 8?
	Have	you	been here before?
	Could	you	send the files?

Questions which ask about the subject:

If we ask a question about the subject we don't need an auxiliary.

Example: What happened?   Who sent the invoice?

'Comment' questions

These are often just one or two words and rely on intonation more than structure to show their meaning. The intonation goes up at the end to show surprise or interest.

Example: A: Roger's been working here for more than 20 years.

B: Has he? / Really?

Question tags

Question tags are very common in spoken English. They can be used either to check information or to confirm what the speaker already knows. The purpose of the question is shown by the intonation.

If the voice rises at the end, this indicates the speaker is not sure and so wants to check the information.

Example: The invoice isn't overdue, is it?

If the voice falls at the end, this indicates the speaker is sure and so is only confirming what he or she already knows.

Example: The invoice isn't overdue, is it?

Unit 6: Reporting verbs

When we report speech in English, we often use different verbs, depending on the **function** of the statement or question.

For example, 'I'll call you back first thing' is a *promise*, so we can say:

Example: He *promised* to call her back.

Many typical reporting verbs follow this construction (verb + *to* + infinitive).

refuse → He refused to stay in the hotel another night.

offer → She offered to work overtime to finish the job.

agree → The company agreed to improve the working conditions.

ask → He asked to have a day off.

Some verbs have a similar construction, but include a direct object (verb + object + *to* + infinitive).

encourage → She encouraged us to talk to her about any difficulties we had with the project.

ask → I asked my colleague to help me.

tell → I told my colleague not to worry about the report.

Other common reporting verbs are *thank*, *apologise* and *deny*.

These follow different constructions.

thank → The Chairman thanked everyone for coming. (verb + object + *for* + *ing*)

apologise → He apologised for keeping them waiting. (verb + for + *ing*)

deny → He denied sharing confidential information with their competitor. (verb + *ing*)

Unit 7: Present perfect simple and present perfect continuous

Both the present perfect simple and the present perfect continuous can be used to refer to past actions which have a present result, or actions which started in the past and continue to the present.

However, there are some differences.

Present perfect simple

The present perfect simple is often used:

- to talk about an activity which is completed
  We've emailed all the customers on the database.
- to talk about something which affects the present in some way
  The machine's *broken* down so we've *had* to stop production.
- to ask about an amount
  How many times *have* you *visited* the Hong Kong office?

Present perfect continuous

The present perfect continuous is often used:

- to talk about something which is still continuing now
  Our market share *has been increasing* steadily over the last few years.
- to ask about the length of time
  How long *have you been studying* English?
- to emphasise the activity more than the result
  Our company *has been producing* that model for a number of years.

Note: There are some verbs (*state verbs*) which we do not use in the continuous form: *know*, *agree*, *like* and *belong*.

Example: He's belonged to the management team for 3 years (not *He's been belonging*...)

Sometimes you need both the simple and continuous form in the same sentence.

Example: We've been working with them for years and we've never had any problems.

Example: I've been living here since January and I've only just met my neighbours!

Unit 8: Future perfect and future continuous

We use the future perfect to talk about an event or action that we think will happen or be completed before a specific point in the future.

Complete market research
Now ——————————✕——————————▶
       Next week

Example: We'll have completed the market research by next week.

We often use the future perfect when talking about deadlines and schedules. The following time expressions are very common when using the future perfect:

- *by the end/beginning of* the week, month
  Example: The company will have announced the financial results by the end of March.
- *already/before*
  Example: We'll have already contacted all the clients before we send them the questionnaires.

We use the future continuous to talk about an event or action which will be in progress in the future.

Work overtime
Now ——————————————————————▶
       Next week

Example: They'll be working a lot of overtime next week.

We can use the future continuous to talk about future plans – in this case, it is similar to present continuous.

Example: We'll be launching a new product next month.

The following time expressions are very common when using the future continuous:

- *this time tomorrow, next* week, year etc.
  Example: This time next year we'll be setting up the new office in Tokyo.
- *in a* month's, year's *time*
  Example: We'll be handing over the project in a month's time.
- *during, in* the next month
  Example: We won't be organising any more training during the next two weeks.

Unit 9: Conditionals

The table on page 85 of the Student's Book gives a summary of the main conditional forms and their uses. Below are some additional modals and verb forms which are also used in conditionals.

Form	Meaning	Examples
(Second /Third Conditionals)		
If + past simple / **past perfect** could + have + infinitive / **past participle**	This is /was one of a number of possibilities.	If we <u>wanted</u> to target a younger market, we <u>could use</u> social networking sites. If I <u>had seen</u> him at the meeting, I <u>could have talked</u> to him about it.
should + **have** + infinitive/**past participle**	This is/was a logical deduction or obligation	If the company <u>used</u> the 4Cs approach, it <u>should improve</u> their customer relations. If he <u>had wanted to leave</u> by the end of the month, he <u>should have told</u> the company earlier.

Form	Meaning	Examples
might + **have** + infinitive/**past participle**	There is/was a small possibility that this would have happened.	If we <u>closed</u> our physical store, we <u>might lose</u> loyal customers. **If we <u>had launched</u> the product earlier, we <u>might not have run</u> into so many difficulties.**
(Mixed) **Past condition, present result**		
If + past perfect / could + infinitive	This is one of a number of possibilities.	If the market had expanded last year, we could increase production.
might + infinitive **Present hypothetical condition, past result**	There is a small possibility that this could happen.	If we had carried out more research, we might not be in this position today.
If+ past simple or continuous/ could + have + past participle	This is one of a number of options we had in the past.	If we were trying to get into that market, we could have opened an office there.
should + have + past participle	This was a logical deduction or obligation about a past result.	If he was the last to leave, he should have checked everything was safe.
might + have + past participle	This was a small possibility for an event in the past.	If we were going to expand the department, we might have taken on more staff.

Unit 11: Gerunds

The gerund looks like the present participle of the verb (the *ing* form) and is used like a noun.

 Example: I really enjoy *working* with my new colleagues.

The gerund is often used after a preposition or noun/adjective/verb + preposition phrase.

 Example: After *graduating* from university, I applied for several jobs abroad.

 Example: I'm responsible for *overseeing* client accounts.

 Example: We really need to concentrate on *improving* our customer feedback process.

 Example: As a result of *implementing* the new system, we've saved a lot of money.

The gerund can be used at the start of a sentence to add emphasis.

 Example: *Working* abroad can be a very interesting experience.

(This sentence could also be written 'It can be a very interesting experience to work abroad.')

Some verbs can only be followed by the gerund form.

 Example: I enjoy *working* with people from different countries.

Some verbs can only be followed by the gerund or the infinitive (without *to*) and there is little difference in meaning.

 Example: They continued *to advertise* the product, even though it was out of production.

Or Example: They continued *advertising* the product, even though it was out of production.

The verbs *like, love, prefer* and *hate* can be followed by either the gerund or the infinitive. Using the infinitive suggests something is a good or bad idea.

 Example: I prefer *to get* my reports done well in advance of the deadline.

Using the gerund shows how you feel about something.

 Example: I prefer *travelling* business class on long-haul flights.

Some verbs can be followed by a gerund or an infinitive and there is a very strong change in meaning. The main verbs in this category are: *stop, remember, forget, regret.*

 Example: I stopped *asking* my colleagues for help with the computer after I took a course. (= I no longer ask them)

 Example: I stopped *to ask* my colleague for help with the computer. (= I was doing something else and I stopped *in order to* ask for help)

Verbs (or phrases) which must take infinitive:	need, ought, want, expect, hope, refuse, agree, can't afford
Verbs (or phrases) which must take gerund form:	(dis)approve of, to be keen on, to be interested in, dislike, enjoy, to be responsible for, don't mind, to be good at, look forward to, avoid, finish, suggest, recommend, to be worth
Verbs which can take either, but change meaning:	stop, regret, forget, remember, try, attempt
Verbs which can take either without changing meaning:	begin, start, continue, intend, love, prefer, hate, like, advise

Unit 12: *Used to*, *be used to* and *get used to*

Used to

- *Used to* as an active verb describes a situation which was a *past habit*.
- *Used to* is followed by the infinitive of the verb.
- The question form is *'Did you use to … ?'*
- The negative form is *'I didn't use to …'*

Example: They used to make those products by hand, but it's all done by machine now.

Example: Did you use to live in Singapore?

Example: We didn't use to use the SAP system.

Be used to and get used to

- *Used to* as an adjective describes a *present situation*.
- If *used to* is followed by a verb, the *ing* form is used.
- The question form is *'Are you used to…?'*
- The negative form is *'I'm not used to…'*

Example: The team is used to setting very high targets.

Example: Is he used to the new system yet?

Example: She's not used to driving on the left yet.

- We use *be used to* when the situation is *already* familiar.
Example: I'm used to starting work at 7am because I work in the production plant.

- We use *get used to* when we the situation is *becoming* familiar.
Example: I'm sure we'll get used to the new office layout soon.

Unit 13: Phrases with prepositions

There are many phrases in English with prepositions. Often, the preposition is dependent on the verb, noun or adjective and so it is easier to learn the whole phrase together as the preposition will always be the same when it is with that particular part of speech.

The table below shows some of the most common phrases, but there are many more.

Verbs with dependent prepositions
agree on (as part of the decision-making process), agree with (a person/proposal), apologise for, (dis)approve of, concentrate on, deal with, depend on, insist on, invest in, object to, specialise in, succeed in
Nouns with dependent prepositions
benefit to, chance of, contrary to, damage to, dealings with, delay in, difficulty in, influence on, intention of, question of, reason for, restrictions on/to, result of, solution to, success with
Adjectives with dependent prepositions
angry about/at/with, aware of, concerned about with, conscious of, convinced of, disappointed at/in/with, essential for/to, familiar with, ignorant of, incapable of, interested in, involved in, opposed to, responsible for, satisfied with, superior to, typical of

Many of these expressions are followed by the gerund form (see Unit 11).

The company specialises in providing high quality adhesives to the construction industry.

Unit 14: Narrative tenses

The following tenses are particularly common when we are telling anecdotes and narrating stories:

Past simple   Past perfect   Past continuous   Historic present

Sometimes we use the *past continuous* with the *past simple* to show when an action is interrupted.

Example: I was coming home from work when the car broke down.

We use the *past perfect* when we have two actions in the past and we want to show which action happened first. We use the past simple to show the more recent past action.

Example: I had always worked full time until I lost my job last year.

We use the *historic present* to add dramatic effect to a narrative.

Example: I was running through the park and I see this man and he starts running after me …

Example: I was talking to my boss the other day and he says we need to start thinking about this new training programme and who's going on it …

Progress test 1: Units 1–5

1 Look at the information about Estée Lauder's life. Complete the text with the correct verb from the box below. Put the verbs in the correct form.

1908	Born
1924	New Way Laboratories founded
1947	Estée Lauder Inc founded
1948	First retail account at Saks Fifth Avenue Department Store, New York
1953	First fragrance
1968	Revenues of $40 million
1972	Son Leonard becomes president. Lauder becomes chair
1995	Company launched on stock market
2004	Dies

launch   reach   hold   decide   sell   grow   take over
set up   work   win

Estée Lauder was born Josephine Esther Mentzer in Queens, New York in 1908. Her uncle, Dr Schotz, was a chemist who **1** _____ his company, New Way Laboratories, in 1924. The company made a variety of products, including several beauty treatments. While Lauder **2** _____ her uncle's products in the shops, she **3** _____ to set up her own company in 1947. By 1948, she **4** _____ her first retail account at Saks Fifth Avenue. In 1953, the company **5** _____ its first fragrance, Youth Dew, and by 1968 the company's revenues **6** _____ $40 million. By the 1960s, Lauder's son, Leonard **7** _____ for the company and in 1972 he **8** _____ as president. Although the company went public in 1995, the family still hold a significant proportion of the shares and several family members **9** _____ key positions since that time. The company that Estée Lauder founded **10**_____ to a multi-million-dollar corporation which now controls over 45% of the cosmetics market in US department stores.

	/20

2 Put the words in the correct order to make sentences using future and modal verb forms.

1 environment will need a we make the definitely priority to.

_____

2 offices might have more we I 'virtual' suppose.

_____

3 even use only business teleconferencing stop may we trips and.

_____

4 Africa going certainly to we develop are in India markets and.

_____

5 extend well further the might Eurozone.

6 A: What's happened to the computer?
   B: it think crashed must I have.

7 A: We're not going to meet the deadline!
   B: extra in asked we last have for should time the meeting.

_____

8 A: Where's Mike?
   B: the gone dentist might he have to.

_____

	/8

3 Complete the gaps with the correct words from the box.

goals   incentives   base-salary   shareholder value
equity-based   cash flow   programme   product-revenue
profit   retention rates

1 As a result of good operating _____ generation, we ended the year with total reserves of $55.0m.

2 This strategy is delivering results as the group continues to register strong performance in customer _____ and acquisition across its whole product range.

3 The shares have fallen from $40 to around $7, which represents a loss in _____ of $60 billion.

4 The company's compensation _____ has come under scrutiny from the financialregulators.

5 The survey argues that setting stretch _____ can be a waste of time if they are not followed up properly.

6 Whilst there are drawbacks to using cash _____ , it is still a useful way to motivate certain types of employees.

7 The engineering group has bounced back into an operating _____ after improving margins this year.

8 Experts say that although disclosure of _____ awards is subject to regulations, it is not straightforward.

	/8

4 Complete the gaps in the conversation between two colleagues.

A: Hi Mike, where are you?

B: I'm on the train, but it's running late. **1** _____

_____ _____ you to do something for me?

A: Yeah, sure, what do you need?

B: Can you print off copies of the agenda for the meeting today?

A: No problem. You're not going to be late for the meeting,

2 _____ _____?

B: Well, I might be. **3** _____ _____ _____

postpone it till 10, then I'll definitely be there?

	/8

5 Read the two job advertisements and complete the gaps. Some letters have been given to help you.

Do you have **1** c_____y (10 letters) and an eye for detail? Can you **2** i_____t (9 letters) your ideas practically and work well in a team? We are a small design company, with a friendly **3** a_____e (10 letters), looking for a new recruit, someone with a lively **4** p_____y (11 letters) and plenty of self-motivation. We can offer you training and a good basic **5** p_____e (7 letters) as well as some long-term **6** i_____s (10 letters), such as share options.

Chief Executive

City of London

7 P_____e (11 letters) related pay up to £150,000 p.a. Our company is a great UK success story which enhances economic growth, employment, **8** i_____n (10 letters) – development of new ideas – and enterprise. You will be a highly skilled communicator, showing excellent **9** i_____n (11 letters) with both colleagues and senior management, facilitating **10** c_____e (11 letters) between differing interest groups. You will be responsible for a **11** b_____t (6 letters) of about £30,000 and be in charge of a **12** d_____t (10 letters) of 150 people.

	/12

6 Complete each gap by writing the correct form of the words given in brackets at the end of the sentence.

1 The industry has been _____ by one or two key players. (large / monopoly)

2 The company was found to have _____ by demanding payments from suppliers to be placed on a 'preferred' list. (act / legal)

3 The banking industry has become much more _____ since the financial crisis. (heavy / regulate)

4 We have become _____ since our acquisition by P&G. (increase / global)

5 Last year the company _____ in new equipment which has significantly increased our production rates. (invest / heavy)

6 There's a variety of _____ structures, such as hierarchical or centralised, which experts have identified in different companies. (organise)

7 The company is _____ its policy on employee promotion after the unions raised objections to the current system. (consider)

8 The company's stock price fell sharply after it was revealed that they were using _____ products in their so-called 'natural' range. (gene / modify)

	/14

7 In each sentence there is one incorrect word. <u>Underline</u> the incorrect word and write the correct word at the end of the sentence.

1 We offer an extra bonus pay after two years of service.

_____

2 My wage is paid monthly into my bank account. _____

3 The new job has a lot of benefits including a company car and an expensive account. _____

4 We're very proud of our organical range of products.

_____

5 If a few firms dominate the market, this is known as a monopoly.

_____

	/10

TOTAL MARKS	/80

Progress test 2: Units 6–10

1 Complete the gaps with a reporting verb that describes the action. The first letters have been given to help you.

Example: 'That's a good idea, I really think you should try it' <u>encourage</u>

1 'I'm sorry I'm late' a_____
2 'I really appreciate your help with this project' t_____
3 'I did not put false information on my CV' d_____
4 'Let me help you with that' o_____
5 'Yes, we can send it express delivery' a_____
6 'I'll give you the results as soon as I have them' p_____

Now use the verbs to transform the sentences into reported form.

Example: He <u>encouraged</u> me <u>to</u> <u>try</u> my idea.

7 She _____ _____ _____ late.
8 He _____ me _____ _____ with the project.
9 He _____ _____ false information on his CV.
10 She _____ _____ _____ me with it.
11 He _____ _____ _____ it express delivery.
12 He _____ _____ _____ me the results as soon as he had them.

/12

2 Complete the gaps with the correct form of the verb. Choose from the present perfect simple, present perfect continuous, future perfect and future continuous.

A: Hi Taija, how's the new job?
B: Well, I **1** _____ (be) there for three months now and I'm enjoying it. Mostly I **2** _____ (meet) clients and **3** _____ (get) to know my new colleagues.
A: **4** _____ you _____ (work) on any specific projects recently?
B: Yes, actually, I **5** _____ (just start) a consulting job for one of our big clients, an energy company.
A: Oh, that sounds interesting, what will it involve?
B: Well, during the next 2 months we **6** _____ (visit) all the regional offices and talking to all the key staff – so I **7** _____ (spend) a lot of time travelling!

A: Wow – exciting! And when will the project finish?
B: According to the schedule, we **8** _____ (complete) the first stage by the end of July but the whole project **9** _____ (not finish) until this time next year, so it's a long way off!

/9

3 Complete the gaps in each sentence with the correct form of the verb in brackets.

1 If we _____ (be) more careful with spending at the beginning of the year, we _____ (not have to) make so many cuts now.
2 The company _____ (not make) as much profit this year if our competitors _____ (not go) bankrupt.
3 He _____ (not be able) to change jobs next year unless he _____ (complete) the course.
4 If we _____ (buy) from anther supplier, we _____ (not be) in such a difficult position now.
5 We _____ (never agree) to those terms if we _____ (realise) that it would be so expensive.
6 If we _____ (fix) the prices at the start of the year, we _____ (not have) so many problems later on.

/12

4 Choose the correct option from the choices in brackets to complete the sentences.

1 If you were in the office on Saturday, you _____ the alarm after you left. (could have setted / should have set)
2 If we had put in a lower bid, we _____ the contract, but I don't think it was only about price. (might have won / should have won)
3 We _____ more time on this point if we had started the meeting earlier. (could have spent / should have spent)
4 The company _____ the new office if they had known about all the planning restrictions. (should not have built / might not have built)

/4

5 Complete the gaps with the correct preposition.

1 Unfortunately, his initial enthusiasm for the job petered _____ as he began to realise how much work was involved.

2 I think we should spend a bit of time screening _____ any applications which are clearly unsuitable.

3 It looks like we've run _____ trouble with the latest prototype: I think we'll have to rethink the design.

4 This presentation offers us a window _____ opportunity to make an impression on some of the biggest names in the business.

5 The company attributed its success _____ a clear strategy and the dedicated attitude of all the staff.

6 Now we've all done the training course, the next stage is to put it _____ practice.

/6

6 Choose the best alternative from the words in brackets to complete the sentences.

1 In order to _____ (give / create / stand) a chance _____ (of / to) winning the contract, we have to put together a really competitive bid.

2 The annual employee survey aims to _____ (have / create / give) everyone a chance _____ (to / for) tell us what they think.

3 I think we should deal with this now in order to _____ (raise / resolve / avoid) a problem _____ (between / within) employees and management later on.

4 We see this merger as a great opportunity to _____ (seek / create) synergy _____ (with / among / between) our two companies.

5 The new regulations are designed to _____ (inhibit / lack / enhance) transparency _____ (in / among / between) the industry.

6 Before we give up completely, I think we should be sure we _____ (seize / explore / seek) every opportunity _____ (to / for) an agreement.

/12

7 Choose the best word from the box to complete the sentences below.

rapport   however   pilot   slash   undertake   gather
tackle   boost

1 The first stage in the project is to _____ a survey in order to _____ as much information as we can.

2 The _____ stage is essential as it allows us to _____ the thorny issues which could cause problems

when we roll out the system to the whole group.

3 Creating a good _____ in the work environment is vital. _____ , it's not always easy to achieve.

4 The consultants have suggested that if we want to _____ our customer ratings, we should _____ delivery times, so that the whole process is much quicker.

/8

8 Choose the best alternative from the words given in brackets to complete the word collocations.

1 Our company has 15 retail _____ (outlets / operators / consumers) and our virtual _____ (outlet / store / media) online.

2 This is an example of a traditional bricks _____ (outlet / store / retailer) whose target _____ (mix / consumers / database) tend to walk in off the street.

3 I think we should really start to integrate the use of social _____ (outlets / marketing / media) into our campaigns, as part of the whole marketing _____ (mix / perspective / retailer).

4 Using database _____ (mix / marketing / operators) will really help us to understand the customer's perspective.

/7

9 Complete each gap by writing the correct form of the word given in brackets at the end of the sentence.

1 The survey tested brand _____ and found that, although most consumers had heard of our company, they had very different _____ of our brands. (aware, perceive)

2 By keeping consistent style, we have been able to achieve the same _____ look for our products – from clothing to the brand _____ of rugs and furniture. (icon, extend)

3 Our services include web _____ – making sure your website is easy to use, and customer _____ marketing – helping you to build contacts with customers. (optimum, relate)

4 As a company, we feel _____ is a core value: we want to keep our systems and processes as _____ as possible. (transparent, complicate)

5 Our new autumn range offers you _____ colours and _____ style. (inspire, afford)

/10

TOTAL MARKS	/80

Progress test 3: Units 11–15

1 Complete the sentences with the correct prepositions from the box.

| in for of for on of of of |

1 The basic prerequisite _____ installing the software is Windows.

2 We're convinced that we can rise to the challenge _____ developing a product which will solve this problem.

3 Unfortunately, none of the candidates have experience _____ dealing with these kinds of situations.

4 As a result _____ creating a website, we've had more business.

5 We'd be very interested _____ working with you to set up a branch here in Almaty.

6 We always have to follow a strict method _____ calculating our risks for every project.

7 As part of the new strategy, we have to focus _____ keeping everyone informed about new projects within the company.

8 As a company, we're very good _____ planning, but we need to transform that into positive action.

| | /8 |

2 Change the following sentences so that they start with the gerund form.

1 The most important thing is to listen to our customers' feedback.
_____ to our customers' feedback _____
_____ _____ important thing.

2 Our main priority is to ensure our customers are protected whenever they need to be.
_____ our customers are protected whenever they need to be _____ _____ _____ priority.

3 It's stressful to commute long distances on a regular basis.
_____ long distances on a regular basis _____
_____ .

| | /3 |

3 Choose the correct verb (*used to*, *be used to* or *get used to*) to complete the sentences. You may need to change the form of the verb.

1 We'd had the old system for ten years and I _____ it. Now they've introduced this new one, don't think I'll ever _____ it.

2 We (not) _____ have breakfast meetings until the company was taken over by an American firm and I (not) _____ it yet.

3 Our offices have relocated to outside the city. I _____ have a short journey to work before, but now I _____ to the longer journey: I listen to music and prepare work for the day.

| | /6 |

4 Match the words from the column on the left with the column on the right to make common phrases with prepositions.

1 (to) look	a of interest
2 (to) be conscious	b on the situation
3 (an) amount	c in their procedures
4 (to) be integrated	d at costs
5 (to) have an impact	e into the system
6 (to) be transparent	f of the risks

| | /6 |

5 Complete the sentences with the phrases from exercise 4.

1 We need to be _____ when entering a new market.

2 The company was told they had to _____ in the future as there had been complaints about unfair treatment in the past.

3 The new committee has been set up to _____ and ways of cutting them.

4 We want these new core values to _____ so that they become part of everything we do.

5 We'll have to wait until we get the test results as they will obviously _____ .

6 I don't know the _____ I'll have to pay for the loan.

| | /6 |

6 Complete the text with the correct form of the verbs in brackets. You can choose from the following tenses: past simple, past perfect, past continuous, historic present.

The worst hotel I ever **1** _____ (stay) in was in London. My company **2** _____ (book) it because I **3** _____ (visit) our office there. When I arrived, I wanted to do was to take a shower as I **4** _____ (have) a long day, but there was no hot water! Anyway, when I called reception to complain, the receptionist **5** _____ (say) 'Just wait half an hour!'. So, I **6** _____ (sit) there waiting when the maintenance man knocked at the door. He said reception **7** _____ (tell) him to come and fix a faulty shower in the room that morning, but he **8** _____ (not have) time until now! By this time, I was really tired, so I went to reception and asked for another room. When the receptionist said I would have to wait while they got another room ready, I got angry and said I **9** _____ (not wait) anymore. So, I **10** _____ (leave) before the first night!

	/10

7 Complete each gap by writing the correct form of the word given in brackets at the end of the sentence.

1 We didn't spend enough on _____ last year, so we'll have to buy some new equipment this year. (maintain)

2 The government are offering tax reductions and interest-free loans to _____ businesses to relocate here. (incentive)

3 Nowadays, a lot of people prefer to use electronic _____ systems rather than road maps. (navigate)

4 We want our business to grow _____ – we don't want to become too big too quickly. (sustain)

5 We need to _____ on this gap in the market and get the product out as quickly as possible. (capital)

6 The change in the rules for _____ of buildings and equipment meant that the company had higher-than-expected losses. (depreciate)

7 The government has introduced cuts in benefits which other parties say will _____ part-time workers. (penalty)

8 When he started the company, his father acted as a _____ for the original bank loan of €5,000. (guarantee)

9 Cheques are considered less safe than direct transfers as some cash offices, allow anyone, not just the _____ , to cash them. (pay)

10 The company was forced to cut jobs after orders dropped and loan _____ increased. (pay)

	/10

8 Complete the sentences with the correct words.

1 Being able to work flexitime has really helped my w_____-_____ b_____ – I can take time off when I need to for the family.

2 What we want to do now is brainstorm to c_____ u_____ w_____ ideas for the new advertising campaign.

3 The company changed its p_____ p_____ after criticism that suppliers had to pay to go on a 'preferred' list.

4 The chairman stressed that this was a new beginning for the company, a time to m_____ f_____ in the right direction after all the previous difficulties.

5 Although some parts of the country have a very low p_____ d_____ , there is still a good infrastructure serving people's basic needs.

6 We value your input and we take the results of the survey very seriously, it's not just a b_____-_____ e_____ .

7 The government announced that, they were finally going to be able to put the ideas i_____ p_____ .

8 We don't want to rush into things, just to be the first in the market – I want to t_____ t_____ over the decision.

	/7

9 Look at the stages of a strategic planning process with their definitions and complete the gaps. The first letters have been given to help you.

1 c_____ Talk to everyone involved to get their ideas

2 e_____ Decide which ideas are useful

3 s_____ Clearly identify which areas to focus on

4 d_____ Build up the strategy

5 i_____ Put the strategy into practice

6 m_____ Check and observe the system

7 e_____ Make sure the system is working

8 Finally, make sure you don't d_____ from the agreed plan.

	/8

10 Choose the words from the group in brackets which make an appropriate phrasal verb to fit in the sentence.

1 (put, get, on, up, with) The boss doesn't _____ anyone arriving late for meetings, no matter what the reason is.

2 (came, took, over, on, off) Demand for this product really _____ after a famous celebrity was seen using it.

3 (put, take, off, up, away) Although the meeting was scheduled for today, we've had to _____ it _____ because so many people couldn't make it.

4 (put, took, away, over, with) After we _____ our rivals in 2008, we gained the largest market share.

5 (put, get, off, away, down) I only had to _____ 5% of the price as a deposit and they've agreed to keep it for me.

6 (put, come, with, over, through) We've had a difficult year, but I think we've _____ it now.

	/16

	TOTAL MARKS	/80

Audio scripts

1 Competitive environment

 2–4 Building relationships across companies See pages 147–148 of the Student's Book.

Making your feelings understood, exercise 1

 5

1 The meeting was interesting.
2 The meeting was interesting.
3 The meeting was interesting.
4 The meeting was interesting.

Making your feelings understood, exercise 2

6

1 The new product is going to be great.
2 They haven't followed the brief.
3 I think he's on the way.
4 The meeting has been cancelled.
5 We haven't received our copy of the contract.

Making your feelings understood, exercise 3

 7

1 **Speaker 1:** Who was at the meeting?
  Speaker 2: Well, Arben was there, but Nora wasn't.
2 **Speaker 1:** How was the course?
  Speaker 2: Well, the course was interesting, but the venue was terrible.
3 **Speaker 1:** What did you think of the new restaurant?
  Speaker 2: The food was good, but there wasn't much choice.
4 **Speaker 1:** What was Paris like?
  Speaker 2: We really enjoyed all the sightseeing, but the weather was awful!

Sounding friendly in informal situations, exercise 2

8

1 Was the meeting OK?
2 It was really frustrating, actually.
3 We were there for two hours and we didn't decide much.
4 Do you want a coffee?
5 I'm afraid I haven't got time, I've got another meeting!
6 Oh no, maybe we can have one later?

2 Future uncertainty

 9–10 Presenting a case at a meeting See pages 149 of the Student's Book.

Discourse markers, exercise 3

11

OK, let's get started.

Right – this is our proposed change – the new product. We wanted to have something new and fresh to present to the market this spring and we think it's time to change our image.

So, as you probably know, this product has been in the pipeline for some time now, and I'd like to give you some information on it … I mean, if we stick with the same type of products we've always had, I think we're going to get left behind, so although there is a risk changing the product, I think it's necessary … So, what do we do now? Well, we've already done some market research which suggests …

3 Rewarding performance

 12–13 Negotiating a pay rise See pages 150–151 of the Student's Book.

Vague language, exercise 1

14

1 We might have to develop something that's performance related.
2 I actually thought that, you know, the performance review was linked to sort of salary.
3 I was also doing the second job, if you see what I mean.
4 It'll probably take about 3 weeks.

Vague language, exercise 3

15

1 **A:** I've sort of got behind with the schedule, so you know …
  B: So what you're saying is you need more time to finish the project?
2 **A:** I think we need to look at working conditions and all that kind of thing.
  B: By 'that kind of thing' do you mean salary and holidays?
3 **A:** It'll probably be ready in about 3 weeks.
  B: Are you sure?
4 **A:** We might not get an answer straight away.
  B: So you mean we'll have to wait?

4 Fostering creativity

16–17 Decision-making See pages 151–152 of the Student's Book.

Evaluative metaphors and idioms, exercise 2

18

Hitesh: OK, so we need to look at the budget for next year and how the department's spending plans fit in …
Iona: Well, can I just say, I think the budget we've been given is completely unreal, I mean how do they expect …?
Hitesh: Hold on, Iona, let's take it a step at a time … Dave?

Dave: Well, I've been looking at our spending on new equipment, for example and …
Iona: Oh no, don't say you're going to cut that – it'd be absolute madness!
Dave: No, what I'm saying is because we've already got solid plans for replacing equipment, I don't think we should cut that. But I do think we could look at cutting some of the maintenance contracts …
Hitesh: OK, well – Iona, any reactions?
Iona: Yeah, actually, that's a good way forward. Do you want me to see what I can do there? Because, I mean, what we're paying now in maintenance costs is stupid …
Hitesh: I'd really welcome that, Iona, and Dave, if you could have a look at some of the other cost …

Evaluative metaphors and idioms, exercise 4

19

1 **Speaker 1:** Well, we could always cut back on overtime …
  Speaker 2: Yes, that's a good way forward. Let's look into that.
2 **Speaker 1:** The suppliers want to double the prices.
  Speaker 2: That's absolute madness! How can they justify that?
3 **Speaker 1:** Would you like me to contact the clients and discuss it?
  Speaker 2: I'd really welcome that. Thanks.
4 **Speaker 1:** The quality is great, but the suppliers just don't seem flexible on delivery times.
  Speaker 2: Don't worry. I'm sure we'll find a way around it.
5 **Speaker 1:** Do you think we could contact the client and ask for an extension?
  Speaker 2: I really have an issue with going back to the client and asking for more time.

5 Organisational cultures

20–22 Dealing with problems across departments See pages 153–154 of the Student's Book.

Strategically summarising a position, exercise 3

23

1 I think *it's mostly about* staff morale.
2 *I'm not saying that.* I think they work very hard.
3 I think the sales team need to change their attitude, *which is what I said.*
4 I agree but *I just think* there may be other reasons.
5 *What I'm saying* is that no one seems to take responsibility.
6 *My point is* that we have to think about cost.

6 Working across cultures

🎧 25–26 **International team-building** See pages 154–155 of the Student's Book.

The stages of building a team and using metaphors in business, exercise 2

🎧 26

1 **Mark:** So I think here I definitely need something to be able to say to my to confirm with head office we're going to go ahead and do this checking.
2 **Mark:** You could probably have done it every two months and kept things moving.
3 **Mark:** Did we go over the top at Staines by checking it every month?
4 I think we should move on from that point now or we'll never finish this meeting.
5 Unfortunately, the business has been going nowhere since Dan retired.
6 Well, it's good to see things are moving forward again now.
7 Sorry, could you go over that again, I'm completely lost.

The stages of building a team and using metaphors in business, exercise 4

🎧 27

1 Can we move on to the next point?
2 I'm afraid I'm completely lost. Could we just recap where we are?
3 I'm pleased to say we can go ahead with the project now.
4 I think we went over the top on the analysis and lost time.
5 Let's try to keep things moving with this if we can.
6 We're moving forward at a rapid rate now.

7 Change management

🎧 28–30 **External negotiating** See page 156 of the Student's Book.

Organising spoken language – head, body, tail, exercise 3

🎧 31

1 You know there may be an alternative way of doing it you know what I mean?
2 Basically there's no black-and-white answer to that as far as I'm concerned.
3 Well I mean I would really welcome that if you see what I mean.
4 In my opinion that doesn't give us enough cover does it?
5 I see what you mean but I just think it's one of those things where they'll always find an excuse don't you?
6 So it doesn't necessarily mean we have to start again right?
7 Well I think we should go ahead with it OK?
8 Erm we need to get things started as soon as possible you know what I mean?

8 Project management

🎧 32 **Maintaining relationships** See page 157 of the Student's Book.

Signalling identities through 'we', exercise 1

🎧 33

Ron: So, we've been going through the schedules and we're probably going to need a bit more time to complete the project. I mean, we're not …
Torsten: But I thought we'd discussed this the last time we met and you said that was the last extension you'd be asking for.
Ron: Look, we all want the project to be a success …
Sylvia: Yes, and we don't want our name associated with something which isn't absolutely top quality …
Dev: Neither do we!
Sylvia: … so what I was going to say was, maybe we shouldn't worry so much about a couple of extra weeks as long as we get this finished to the highest specifications.
Ron: You're right: and of course we don't want to overrun by months as we've already started planning the grand opening …
Torsten: OK, how about the costs – what are we talking about here – are we going to be massively over our budget?
Dev: I don't think so – the sub-contractors are on a fixed price, so the extra time shouldn't impact on the price and if we can put a bit of pressure on them, I'm sure we can get it down to a couple of weeks, maximum …
Sylvia: OK, because we can't push our budget any further …
Ron: And we wouldn't want you to – we really value your sponsorship and I think we've worked together really well so far …

9 E-marketing

🎧 34–35 **Organising a presentation** See pages 158–159 of the Student's Book.

Delivering an e-presentation, exercise 1

🎧 34

Hi my name is Philip Weiss and I'm the managing director of Zn. Over the next five minutes I'll give you a brief introduction of who we are how we can help HQs meet their challenges and what opportunities the Internet created for them and how we developed a methodology to think differently and execute online campaigns and finally we'll look at how we can help you.

Introducing and linking slides, exercise 3

🎧 36

1 How many of you here today have tried this product?
2 Does this problem sound familiar?
3 What is the biggest challenge we're facing today?
4 So how could we solve this problem?
5 Where will our next big market be?
6 So what's the secret of their success?

Introducing and linking slides, exercise 3

🎧 37

Over the next 5 minutes I'll give you a brief introduction to e-marketing.

First let's look at the marketing concept.

Now let's turn to e-market planning.

Moving on now to competitor analysis.

Now I'd like to talk about objective setting.

10 Branding

🎧 38 **Using persuasive communication in meetings** See page 160 of the Student's Book.

The language of persuasion, exercise 1

🎧 39

1 This is not just a good team. This is a fantastic team.
2 Yes, we want the business, but we need to deliver on time.
3 The product won't be an average product. It will be a superb product.
4 This is not just ordinary customer service. This is excellent customer service.
5 Yes, the deadline is important, but quality is more important.
6 This is no ordinary sales campaign, this is revolutionary.
7 People don't just buy our products for what they do, they're buying a lifestyle.
8 Yes, we want to be first in the market, but not if the quality suffers.

Using *if* to persuade and direct staff, exercise 2

🎧 40

1 **a** If you're working on the front desk, you need to greet visitors.
  b If I'm working on the front desk, I always greet visitors.
2 **a** If you're selling a new product, you need to emphasise the benefits.
  b If I'm selling a new product, I always emphasise the benefits.
3 **a** If you're making a follow-up call, you need to make sure the customer is happy.
  b If I'm making a follow-up call, I always make sure the customer is happy.
4 **a** If you're arranging a meeting, you need to book the room in advance.
  b If I'm arranging a meeting, I always book the room in advance.

11 Accounting

🎧 41–42 **Developing internal relationships** See page 161 of the Student's Book.

Polite language, exercise 1

🎧 43

1 I'm afraid I can't make the meeting on Friday.
2 Would it be all right if I kept all the paperwork here?

3 Gosh, you've done it so much more quickly than I could have.
4 Oh, it was nothing, we only spent the whole weekend working on it!
5 You've done a great job! Well done.
6 Can I hold on to this a bit longer? Would that be OK?
7 I'm really grateful for all your support.
8 Sorry, James, I didn't realise you didn't want to be disturbed.

Polite language, exercise 3

🎧 44

Tarja: OK, well, as you know we're about half-way through the changeover between the old accounting system and the new one and it seems to be going really well. I mean you two and the rest of the team have done a great job keeping the project on track.

Piotr: Yes, can I just add that we really appreciate all your hard work, and the fact that you've kept everyone on the team motivated has made a huge difference.

Jan: Oh, it was nothing really, I mean all those weekends of overtime …!

Tarja: No, but seriously, you've done really well and you made it look so easy!

Tove: Well, it was pretty difficult at the beginning and I'm afraid we missed some of the early deadlines, but it seems to have settled down now.

Piotr: What we'd like to find out now is where you think you'd need our support?

Tove: Well, we'll probably need …

12 Microfinance

🎧 45 **Delivering a presentation** See page 162 of the Student's Book.

Use techniques to improve your delivery (stress, chunking and pace), exercise 1

🎧 46

1 First of all I'd like to thank you all for coming today – it's great to see so many people.
2 So who are we and what do we do?
3 We aim to extend credit to some of the world's poorest people to help them to help themselves.
4 Unlike a traditional bank we will visit our customers – we don't expect them to come to us.
5 And there are no charges for late payments and no minimum loan amount.
6 That means anyone at any level can get credit from us.

Use techniques to improve your delivery (stress, chunking and pace) exercise 2

🎧 47

Barack Obama: This is your victory. I know you didn't do this just to win an election and I know you didn't do it for me. You did it because you understand the enormity of the task that lies ahead. For even as we celebrate tonight, we know the challenges that tomorrow will bring are the greatest of our lifetime – two wars, a planet in peril, the worst financial crisis in a century.

Use techniques to improve your delivery (stress, chunking and pace), exercise 3

🎧 48

Muhammad Yunus: The conventional banks are based on one basic principle: the more you have, the more you can get.

We reversed that principle. Our principle is this – the less you have, the more attractive you are for us.

In order to create a completely new bank, we have to get rid of the whole idea of collateral.

We said I don't need anything, I'll just give you a loan.

And that's what we do. We have no collateral. We have no guarantee.

13 Corporate Social Responsibility

🎧 49–51 **Supporting the speaker** See pages 163–164 of the Student's Book.

Supporting the speaker through listener responses, exercise 1 and exercise 2

🎧 52

1 **Speaker A:** I'm not totally happy with the next one.
  Speaker B: Uh-huh. Sure.
2 **Speaker A:** But, you're not actually directly giving money back to the community as such.
  Speaker B: Hmm, maybe.
3 **Speaker A:** Well, I'll change that to 'support' if 'sponsorship' is too strong a word. So that's fine.
  Speaker B: Good. Yes. Absolutely.
4 **Speaker A:** It's not exactly what I had in mind.
  Speaker B: Oh.
5 **Speaker A:** So, you think we can get it done by Friday, yeah?
  Speaker B: [silence]
6 **Speaker A:** I think it'll look great, don't you?
  Speaker B: Uh-huh.
7 **Speaker A:** I'll try and send that off to you a bit later.
  Speaker B: Great.
8 **Speaker A:** I think the team are starting to work really well together.
  Speaker B: Yes, really.

Supporting the speaker through listener responses, exercise 3

🎧 53

Ken: Hi, Sarah. Ken here.
Sarah: Hi, Ken. Good to hear from you. Everything OK?
Ken: Yes, very good. Just calling about sorting out the brochure.
Sarah: Oh.
Ken: It's just that it's not finished at the moment.
Sarah: Hmm.
Ken: But, we also need to try and get down on paper what our mission is as clearly as possible.
Sarah: [silence]
Ken: Do you agree?
Sarah: Maybe. What do you suggest we change?

Ken: Well, there are three headings there. The first one is leadership, then communication and then sustainable tourism, yes?
Sarah: Uh-huh.

14 Strategic planning

🎧 54–56 **Using narratives in interviews** See page 165 of the Student's Book.

Narrative tenses, exercise 1

🎧 57

Of course, when you work in the retail business, you often have funny experiences with customers, but one that I'll always remember was in my first job. I was working as a shop assistant in a very expensive boutique in Milan. It was a Monday and the shop was actually closed, but I had gone in to do some stock-taking. While I was checking the stock, there was a loud knock. So, I walk up to the door and who should be standing there but a very famous football player and his girlfriend! As I had only been in the job a short time, I didn't dare open the shop on my own, so I called my boss. My boss was so shocked at first she couldn't say anything, but then she just shouts 'Open the door, open the door!' So, we ended up opening the shop just for the footballer and his girlfriend, but it was worth it!

Answering questions in interviews, exercise 2

🎧 58

1 Yes, when I first started my present job, all the staff were still doing everything by hand – there were no computers, even for the most basic information tasks. I think the staff really wanted to change, but the managing director, who was also the owner, didn't see the point … So, eventually I was able to go to the manager with all the information and persuade him to invest in computers and so I feel that was a really good achievement.
2 I think, if I want something, nothing will stop me – I mean, for example, we were having a team-building event the other week and we had to complete this outside course, but I'd forgotten my trainers … anyway, I see some trainers just by the door – obviously someone's taken them off to come in, so I just take those and carry on … so, my friends might say I was a bit ruthless, but I think I'm competitive.
3 When my company was taken over last year, I had a new boss, and he insisted that we were all on call all the time. Well, our team had never worked like that before and didn't really see why we should change … in the end, we called a meeting and organised a rota so that only one of us was on call out of hours and that seems to have solved the problem.

Answer key

1 Competitive environment

Vocabulary: Sport as a metaphor for business

1
1 b **2** e **3** c **4** a **5** d
2
1 globalised **2** Perfect **3** largely **4** environment **5** heavily **6** natural

Vocabulary: Adjective and adjective + noun combinations

1
1 political, economic **2** impressive, symbolic **3** legal
4 sustainable, profitable
2
1 politics political **2** economical economic **3** impressing impressive
4 legality legal **5** sustaining sustainable, sustained

Grammar: Tenses that talk about the past

1
1 (set up) **2** (opened) **3** (diversified) **4** (took over) **5** (expanded)
6 (merged) **7** (launched) **8** (sold) **9** (reduced) **10** (announced)
2
1 has operated **2** had already opened, diversified **3** has had
4 was expanding rapidly / expanded rapidly, had opened
5 merged, had already taken over **6** has run
7 had reduced, had already decreased
3
1 haven't seen **2** have been/'ve been **3** saw **4** said **5** went
6 spent **7** haven't had **8** went **9** wasn't **10** have just heard / 've just heard
4
Li Ka Shing's father <u>died</u> when he <u>was</u> just 12 years old, leaving him as head of the family. So, he <u>left</u> school to work in a plastics factory to provide for his family, where he <u>was</u> often <u>working</u> 16-hour days.

His hard work <u>paid</u> off and he <u>went</u> on to start his own plastics manufacturing company called 'Cheung Kong Industries'. The company <u>grew</u> rapidly, and was listed on the Hong Kong Stock Exchange in 1972. Cheung Kong (Holdings) Limited <u>has continued</u> to grow, up to the present day, through acquiring major companies such as "Hongkong Electric Holdings Limited.

Li Ka Shing <u>has moved</u> into many other areas since he <u>started</u> in business, including telecommunications, shipping, financial services and real estate. Forbes business magazine <u>estimated</u> the wealth of Li Ka Shing to be 13 billion US dollars in 2005.

Skills: Making your feelings understood

1
a 2 **b** 4 **c** 1 **d** 3
2
1 e **2** d **3** b **4** a **5** c
3
1 B: Well, <u>Arben</u> was there, but <u>Nora</u> wasn't
2 B: Well, the course was <u>interesting</u>, but the <u>venue</u> was <u>terrible</u>.
3 B: The <u>food</u> was <u>good</u>, but there <u>wasn't</u> much <u>choice</u>.
4 B: We <u>really</u> enjoyed all the <u>sightseeing</u>, but the <u>weather</u> was <u>awful</u>!

Skills: Sounding friendly

1
1 Did you have a good meal out in Aachen?
2 Did you go/sit downstairs or upstairs?
3 Was it good? / Did you have a good time?
4 And was the food great?

2
Suggested answers
1 Was the meeting OK?
2 It was really frustrating, actually.
3 We were there for two hours and we didn't decide much.
4 Do you want a coffee?
5 I'm afraid I haven't got time, I've got another meeting!
6 Oh no, maybe we can have one later?
3
Suggested answers
1 Drink?
2 Coffee please.
3 Journey OK? / Good journey?
4 OK, but – flight was delayed about 45 minutes.
5 Much traffic on the way?
6 No, pretty quiet (actually).

2 Future uncertainty

Vocabulary: STEEP analysis

1
S = Socio-cultural T= Technological E= Economic / Environmental P= Political
F= Fast M= Moving C= Consumer G= Goods
2
1 purchase **2** massive **3** shape **4** conversely **5** organic
6 genetically modified **7** shortages **8** reconsidering
3
1 shortages **2** genetically modified **3** Conversely **4** organic **5** reconsidering
6 shape **7** massive **8** purchase

Vocabulary: Consumer goods sectors

1
1 drink **2** electronics **3** care **4** retail **5** beauty **6** electricals
2
1 health and beauty **2** consumer electronics **3** home care **4** food and drink
5 home electricals **6** Supermarket retail

Grammar: Future certainty and uncertainty

1
1 will **2** could **3** might **4** may **5** will probably **6** will definitely
7 it is highly unlikely that **8** are going to **9** may **10** will
a Possible: 2 ,3, 4, 9   **b Probable:** 5, 7, 10   **c Certain:** 1, 6, 8
2
1 suppose **2** must **3** will **4** highly unlikely **5** looks **6** guess
3
1 B **2** A **3** A **4** B **5** A **6** B

Skills: Discourse markers

1
1 So **2** Well **3** as you can imagine **4** Right **5** So **6** obviously
2
1 So **2** Then **3** Obviously **4** Well **5** mean **6** other hand **7** just
3
4, 2, 5, 1, 3

Reading 1 Food Retail in India

1
1 c **2** d **3** b **4** e **5** a
2
1 F (Food and grocery is the second-largest segment …)
2 Not stated

3 F (Until the late 1990s food retailing was concentrated in the south of the country)
4 T (The cost of real estate in the southern region was less than other regions)
5 T (Changing lifestyles and tastes)
6 T (Increasing disposable income; there is a scarcity of time)
7 F (A huge increase is expected from the corporate players)

3
1 incited by   **2** untapped   **3** fuelled by   **4** come of age   **5** strenuous
6 paving the way   **7** scarcity   **8** have an edge (over)   **9** rivals   **10** poised

4
1 have/has the edge over   **2** poised   **3** pave the way   **4** rivals   **5** untapped
6 Incited by   **7** coming of age   **8** scarcity   **9** fuelled by   **10** strenuous

Writing 1: Preparing presentation slides

1
Suggested answers
1 b   **2** d   **3** a   **4** c

2
Suggested answers
a example given (*Food spending and consumption increasing – opportunity for retailers and service companies*)
b 50 percent private consumption spent on food
c Less time available– convenience shopping needed
d Unbranded products 60 percent of total food bill and increasing
e Food retail – opportunities for corporates to diversify
f Food retail will attract foreign and domestic investment

3
Suggested answers
a example given (*Food spending increasing*)
b Private consumption 50%
c more convenience
d 60% unbranded products
e Opportunities for diversification
f Foreign investment up

4
a The numbers of working women are increasing.
b The retail sector is lacking logistics providers at present.
c In the 1990s, larger retail stores developed.
d In the last tenyears, more hypermarkets have opened.
e In the next ten years, the global players may enter the market.
f The market power of the customers is getting stronger.

Unit 3 Rewarding performance

Vocabulary: Describing earnings

1
1 wage   **2** pay   **3** remuneration   **4** income   **5** reward   **6** salary
2
1 remuneration   **2** pay   **3** reward   **4** wage   **5** income   **6** salary

Vocabulary: Word partnerships with *incentive* and *pay*

1
1 B   **2** A   **3** A   **4** C   **5** B   **6** C   **7** B   **8** A   **9** C   **10** A
2
1 pay   **2** pay   **3** payments   **4** pay, payments   **5** payment

Grammar: Compound nouns

1
1 g   **2** f   **3** b   **4** a   **5** c   **6** d   *wages* is not needed
2
1 annual base salary   **2** customer retention rates
3 short-term cash incentives   **4** operating cash flow
5 increased shareholder value   **6** new product revenue
3
1 stretch   **2** operating   **3** comparison   **4** compensation
5 equity-based   *increase* is not needed
4
1 product revenue   **2** operating profit   **3** base salary   **4** cash incentives

Skills: Vague language

1
1 might have to develop something that's   **2** you know the performance review was linked to sort of   **3** if you see what I mean   **4** It'll probably take about
a **Collaborative:** 2, 3   **b** **Competitive:** 1, 4

2
Suggested answers
1 I'd really like to get a promotion in about 2 years.
2 We might work on that idea in the future.
3 I'm not, you know, happy with the salary and (all) that sort/kind of thing …
4 I've had a sort of increase in my responsibilities – looking after new clients and all that sort/kind of thing.
5 We will probably make some changes to the department in the next few months.

3a
1 So what you're saying is you need more time to finish the project?
2 By 'that kind of thing' do you mean salary and holidays?
3 How sure of that are you?
4 So you mean we'll have to wait?

3b
1 So what you're **saying** is you need more **time** to **finish** the **project**? [voice up at the end of the question]
2 By '**that kind of thing**' do you mean **salary** and **holidays**? [voice up at the end]
3 Are you **sure**? [*sure* could be stressed, voice up at the end]
4 So you **mean** we'll have to **wait**? [voice up at the end]

4
1 So you mean it's not definite?   **3** So, what you're saying is it's behind schedule?
2 How sure of that are you?   **4** So you mean we don't know the date?

4 Fostering creativity

Vocabulary: Word formations connected with creativity

1
1 inventions   **2** creativity   **3** imagination   **4** interaction   **5** convergence
6 divergence   **7** implementation   **8** innovations

2
1 innovator   **2** implementation   **3** Creative   **4** divergent   **5** convergence
6 interactive   **7** inventors   **8** unimaginative

3
1 *imaginary* – imaginative   **2** *converging* – convergence
3 *inventionary* – inventive   **4** *divergement* – divergence
5 *interactiveness* – interactivity   **6** *creativeness* – creation
7 *innovating* – innovative   **8** *implementory* – implementation

Grammar: Past modals

1
1 d   **2** a   **3** b   **4** a   **5** e   **6** c
2
1 d   **2** g   **3** e   **4** a   **5** h   **6** c   **7** b   **8** f
3
1 should have ordered   **2** might have had to   **3** could have booked
4 must have had   **5** shouldn't have shut   **6** can't have seen   **7** must have cost
8 should have changed

Skills: Evaluativ metaphors and idioms

1
1 down   **2** around   **3** balance   **4** on   **5** with   **6** into
Positive: 2, 3   **Negative:** 4, 6, 5
1 is the expression which is neither positive nor negative.

2
1 No   **2** cuts in the maintenance contracts
3 to find out about cutting maintenance contract costs

3
1 completely unreal   **2** absolute madness   **3** solid plans
4 a good way forward   **5** stupid   **6** I'd really welcome that
Positive: 3, 4, 6   **Negative:** 1, 2, 5

4

Suggested answers
1 Yes, <u>that's a good way forward</u>. Let's look into that.
2 That's <u>absolute madness</u>! How can they justify that?
3 I'd <u>really welcome that</u>. Thanks.
4 Don't worry, I'm sure we'll <u>find a way around it</u>.
5 I really <u>have an issue with</u> going back to the client and asking for more time.

Reading 2 Entrepreneurship: two schools of thought

1
2 is the best summary

2
1 F (*It* [the question] *goes to the heart of how we should encourage budding entrepreneurs*)
2 NS ([*entrepreneurs*] *need huge amounts of training and support and learning*) But he doesn't specify money, although this could be included in *support*.
3 T
4 T
5 F (*You are someone who likes being in control of your own destiny rather than just joining a company and climbing your way up the corporate ladder*)
6 F (*There is a danger in encouraging people to become entrepreneurs*)
7 F (*She is in the process of launching two new businesses*)
8 T

3
1 idle curiosity (paragraph 1)   2 budding (paragraph 1)   3 set up (paragraph 6)
4 rebellious streak (paragraph 7)   5 thinks along the same lines (paragraph 10)
6 embed (paragraph 11)

4
1 c   2 f   3 b   4 e   5 g   6 h   7 a   8 d

5
1 tenacity; vital   2 is suited to; drive   3 thinking along the same lines   4 aptitude
5 budding   6 dictate

Writing 2: Describing a process

1
1 has been promoted / was promoted   2 is updated   3 is written
4 are needed   5 are sent   6 must be returned   7 be invited   8 are held
9 can be provided   10 will be requested   11 is appointed   12 is arranged

2
1 C   2 B   3 B   4 A   5 A   6 C   7 A   8 B   9 C   10 C

5 Organisational cultures

Vocabulary: Vocabulary to talk about organisations

1
1 d   2 f   3 e   4 b   5 a   6 c   7 b   'g' is not used

2
1 expense accounts   2 organisational structure   3 reward systems
4 role culture   5 dress code   6 task culture   7 atmosphere at work

3
1 procedures   2 budget   3 norms   4 departments   5 rules   6 values
7 personality

4
1 C   2 B   3 B   4 A   5 C   6 C

Grammar: Asking questions effectively

1
1 Why don't we take a short break?
2 We don't have to finish by 4, do we?
3 Do you know when we're having the launch party?
4 Would you have time to set up the meeting room? / Would you have time to set the meeting room up?
5 Why didn't you send me an email?
6 I was wondering if I could take tomorrow off?
7 Have we – even though we lost that big contract?

2
a 4   b 2   c 7   d 6   e 1   f 5   g 3

3
1 won't he   2 were we   3 hadn't I   4 wouldn't they   5 don't you / shouldn't we
6 didn't they   7 could you   8 shall we

4
1 Really   2 Why didn't   3 Why don't we   4 could you   5 haven't you
6 Could/Can I ask

Skills: Strategically summarising a position

1
1 saying   2 think, honest with   3 mean   4 point   5 talking about   6 means

2
1 it's mostly about   2 which is what I just said   3 not saying that
4 I'm saying is   5 but I just think

3
Suggested answers
1 it's mostly about   2 I'm not saying that   3 which is what I said   4 I just think
6 What I'm saying   7 My point is

6 Working across cultures

Vocabulary: Vocabulary related to culture

1
1 c   2 e   3 g   4 a   5 f   6 b   7 d

Vocabulary: Nouns to make positive and negative judgements

1
1 conflict   2 synergy   3 transparency   4 problem
5 opportunity   6 chance

2

Verbs	Nouns	Prepositions
give/stand/create/have/get	a chance	to/of
raise/resolve/avoid	a conflict /a problem	between / of
seize/explore/exploit	an opportunity	for/to
create/seek	synergy	between/among/with
inhibit/lack/enhance	transparency	in/between
solve/cause/have	a problem	with

3
1 create synergies with   2 seize every opportunity to   3 stand a chance of
4 avoid conflicts between   5 have problems with   6 enhance transparency in

Grammar: Reporting verbs

1
1 apologise   2 agree   3 promise   4 refuse   5 deny   6 encourage   7 thank
8 offer

2
1 encourage   2 promise   3 thank   4 offer   5 agree   6 apologise   7 refuse
8 deny

3
1 encouraged, to apply   2 promised to call   3 thanked, for doing
4 offered to sort   5 agreed to increase   6 apologised for being   7 refused to start
8 denied saying anything

4
1 to work   2 to refund   3 for their continuing   4 offered to give us
5 denied taking   6 me to apply   7 apologised for sending   8 to deliver

Skills: The stages of building a team and using metaphors in business

1
1 forming   2 storming   3 norming   4 performing
Stages to their definitions: a 2   b 1   c 3   d 4

2
1 go ahead **2** kept things moving **3** go over the top **4** move on
5 going nowhere **6** moving forward **7** completely lost
3
a **a desire for progress:** 4   **c** **progress:** 1, 2, 6
b **a lack of progress:** 3, 5, 7
4
Suggested answers
1 move on **2** completely lost **3** go ahead **4** went over the top
5 keep things moving **6** moving forward

Reading 3 Geert Hofstede

1
Hofstede is famous for his 'dimensions' of culture which he identified and for the research he carried out in IBM in different countries. His research is important today because with more businesses becoming global, it helps employees to understand colleagues and customers from many different cultures.
2
1 c **2** d **3** a **4** b
3
2, 4 and 5 are true
4
1 pioneering (paragraph 1) **2** subsequent (paragraph 1)
3 pseudonym (paragraph 1) **4** embrace (paragraph 1) **5** intangible (paragraph 2)
6 reinforced (paragraph 3) **7** equip (paragraph 4) **8** encounter (paragraph 5)
9 conflict (paragraph 5) **10** suitability (paragraph 6)
5
1 e **2** c **3** g **4** a **5** f **6** b **7** d
6
1 encounter, formula **2** insensitivity, conflict **3** distinguish **4** ignorant, equip
5 made up of **6** differentiate **7** pseudonym **8** subsequent

Writing 3: Argument-led writing

1
Pros: help workers negotiate for better wages and conditions, foster teamwork
Cons: raise benefits to unrealistically high levels, can lead to job cuts, create hostile environment, made it difficult for companies to react flexibly
2
Present reasons: since, for the reason that, *because, for, in that, seeing as*
State reason: as a result, *so, so that, therefore*
Make a contrast: while, even though, *but, whilst, although, however*
3
1 because **2** Although **3** seeing as **4** so **5** whilst/while **6** As a result
7 even though **8** in that

7 Change management

Vocabulary: Idiomatic language

1
1 out **2** of **3** limelight **4** take **5** at **6** wrenching **7** thorny **8** into
2
1 take root **2** tackle the thorny issues **3** petered out **4** gut-wrenching
5 craves the limelight **6** ran into trouble **7** window of opportunity
8 at the coalface

Vocabulary: Cohesion and referencing

1
1 d **2** e **3** a **4** b **5** f **6** c
2
1 However **2** Thus **3** those actions **4** they assume
5 That sounds reasonable but **6** Two different groups of people

Grammar: Present perfect simple and continuous

1
1 have been waiting **2** haven't / have not eaten **3** have been redecorating
4 have been trying **5** has asked **6** has not / hasn't said
2
1 have been selling; have not brought **2** have been developing; haven't tested
3 have been waiting; haven't heard **4** has been commuting; has just moved
3
1 How long have/has the company been looking for a new Head Office?
2 How many days holiday have you taken this year?
3 You have made 6 sales since last week.
4 How long have/has the company had the new line?
5 The company have / has been developing the new product since last year.
6 How many rooms have you booked for the conference?

Skills: Organising Spoken Language

1
Head: I think, well, yes, I see, I see what you mean but, right, OK, you know, well, I see what you mean but, I mean, as far as I'm concerned, but, so, yeah, I'm sorry to trouble you, erm, basically, in my opinion
Tail: do you see what I mean, right (with rising intonation), OK (with rising intonation), yeah (with rising intonation), you know what I mean, as far as I'm concerned (up-down intonation), don't you, doesn't it
2
1 Basically, right?   **5** mean, OK
2 I see what you mean   **6** you know, you know what I mean
3 as I'm concerned, see what I mean   **7** Yeah, doesn't it
4 I think, don't you   **8** So, yeah
3
1 You know | there may be an alternative way of doing it | you know what I mean?
2 Basically | there's no black- and- white answer to that | as far as I'm concerned.
3 Well | I mean I would really welcome that | if you see what I mean.
4 In my opinion | that doesn't give us enough cover | does it?
5 I see what you mean | but I just think it's one of those things where they'll always find an excuse | don't you?
6 So | it doesn't necessarily mean we have to start again | right?
7 Well | I think we should go ahead with it | OK?
8 Erm | we need to get things started as soon as possible | you know what I mean?

8 Project management

Vocabulary: Project stages

1
1 undertake **2** put it into practice **3** initial, brief, overview, requirements
Project stages: 5, 3, 1, 4, 6, 2

Vocabulary: Verb/noun combinations for project planning

1
1 unwanted projects **2** the stakeholders **3** teamwork **4** information
5 costs **6** confidence **7** delivery times
2
1 gather information **2** increase confidence **3** slash delivery times
4 screen out unwanted projects **5** Engaging the stakeholders
6 encourage teamwork **7** cut costs

Grammar: Future perfect and future continuous

1
To talk about something in progress in the future (or expected to be in progress in the future): 1, 3, 6
To talk about something that is seen as already completed before a certain time: 2, 4, 5
2
1 will be going through **2** will have received **3** will have announced
4 will be fully upgrading **5** will be investing **6** will have set up
7 will be undergoing **8** will have sorted out
3
1 By the end **2** This time next **3** In 2 months' time **4** By the end
5 In 6 months' time **6** By the end **7** In a year's

Skills: Signalling identities through 'we'

1
1 we're probably going to need **2** we'd discussed this **3** we all want the project
4 Neither do we **5** we get this finished **6** we've already started planning
7 are we talking about here **8** we can put a bit of pressure **9** push our budget
10 we've worked together
2
a Exclusive present / corporate 'we': 1, 4, 6, 8, 9,
b Inclusive present / corporate 'we': 2, 3, 5, 10
c Vague 'we': 7
3
a Exclusive present / corporate 'we': 1, 3, 5, 6
b Inclusive present / corporate 'we': 2, 4
c Vague 'we'

Reading 4 Peter Drucker and his talent to spot trends

1
a 2 **b** Guidance for the future **c** 1 **d** 3
2
1 d **2** a **3** b **4** c
3
Positive: applaud, restore. All the others are negative in this context.
4
1 d **2** f **3** g **4** a **5** h **6** b **7** e **8** c
5
1 c **2** e **3** d **4** a **5** b
6
a 4 **b** 1 **c** 5 **d** 2 **e** 3
7
1 turbulent, public outcry **2** restore, plaguing
3 in the wake of, undermined **4** pave the way **5** applaud

Writing 4: Describing graphs

1
1 T **2** F **3** F **4** T
2
1 virtually **2** completely **3** totally different **4** great deal
5 exactly (the) same as
3
1 The peak in January 2010 is ~~totally~~ the highest on the graph. [*by far*]
2 Between January 2003 and 2004, long-term unemployment levels were ~~quite~~ higher than medium-term levels. [*slightly*]
3 The level of unemployment between 1980 and 1982 is ~~exactly~~ the same as between 1984 and1985. [*virtually/ approximately*]
4 Overall, the long-term unemployment levels are ~~totally~~ different from the medium-term levels. [*not very*]

9 E-marketing

Vocabulary: Marketing and e-marketing terms

1
1 marketing **2** mix **3** producer's **4** customer's **5** Price **6** cost **7** Product
8 wants **9** needs **10** Place **11** convenience **12** promotion
13 communication
2
1 e-tailer **2** pure play **3** bricks, clicks **4** multi-channel **5** search engine
6 social media **7** virtual **8** database
3
1 B **2** A **3** B **4** C **5** A **6** C **7** B **8** B **9** C **10** B

Grammar: Standard and mixed conditionals

1
1 c **2** h **3** a **4** g **5** d **6** f **7** e **8** b
2
1 will mean **2** had followed **3** don't/won't consider
4 wouldn't have spent **5** wanted **6** improve
7 might have had **8** had asked

Skills: Delivering an e presentation

1
Hi / my name is Philip Weiss / and I'm the managing director of Zn. / Over the next five minutes / I'll give you a brief introduction of who we are / how we can help HQs meet their challenges / and what opportunities the Internet created for them / and how we developed a methodology to think differently and execute online campaigns / and finally we'll look at how we can help you.

Skills: Introducing and linking slides

1
■ So what are the **main challenges** facing HQs **today**?

■ So **how** can we **help you**?
Suggested answers
1 How many of you **here today** have tried this **product**?

2 Does this **problem** sound **familiar**?

3 What is the **biggest challenge** we're facing **today**?

4 So how could we **solve** this **problem**?

5 Where will our **next** big **market** be?

6 So what's the **secret** of their **success**?
In general, we go down on the stressed words, but up at the end to signal a question.
2
1 give, brief **2** look at **3** turn to **4** Moving on **5** way, start
6 focus, on **7** talk about **8** interested, look forward
3
1 Over the next five minutes I'll give you a brief introduction to e-marketing
2 First let's look at the marketing concept
3 Now let's turn to e-market planning
4 Moving on now to competitor analysis
5 Now I'd like to talk about objective setting

10 Branding

Vocabulary: Branding expressions

1
1 own **2** manufacturer's **3** luxury **4** licensed **5** image **6** awareness
7 positioning **8** extension
2
1 awareness **2** own **3** manufacturer's **4** image **5** luxury **6** positioning
7 extension **8** licensed **9** repositioning **10** equity

Vocabulary: Describing brands and products

1
1 transmit **2** perceptions **3** gross revenues **4** beyond **5** assets
6 attributed to **7** extensions **8** boost

2
1 physical **2** affordable **3** iconic **4** vibrant **5** relaxed **6** uncomplicated
7 inspirational **8** versatile

3
1 B **2** A **3** A **4** C **5** B **6** C **7** C **8** A

4
1 from by **2** ropes straps **3** base sole **4** unquestionable unmistakable

Skills: The language of persuasion

1
1 This is not just a good team. | This is a fantastic team.
2 Yes, we want the business, | but we need to deliver on time.
3 The product won't be an average product. | It will be a superb product.
4 This is not just ordinary customer service. | This is excellent customer service.
5 Yes, the deadline is important, | but quality is more important.
6 This is no ordinary sales campaign, | this is revolutionary.
7 People don't just buy our products for what they do, | they're buying a lifestyle.
8 Yes, we want to be first in the market, | but not if the quality suffers.

Skills: Using *if* to persuade and direct staff

1
if **to be conditional:** 1, 4, 6, 7
if **to persuade/direct:** 2, 3, 5, 8

2 *Suggested answers*
1 a If you're working on the front desk, you need to greet visitors.
b If I'm working on the front desk, I always greet visitors.
2 a If you're selling a new product, you need to emphasise the benefits.
b If I'm selling a new product, I always emphasise the benefits.
3 a If you're making a follow-up call, you need to make sure the customer is happy.
b If I'm making a follow-up call, I always make sure the customer is happy.
4 a If you're arranging a meeting, you need to book the room in advance.
b If I'm arranging a meeting, I always book the room in advance.

Reading 5 The power of words

1
Sentence 4 is the best summary.
2
1 F **2** T **3** F **4** T **5** T **6** F **7** T
3
1 of **2** in, on **3** from **4** with **5** in **6** by, of **7** on
4
1 d **2** g **3** j **4** c **5** a **6** i **7** h **8** f **9** b **10** e
5
1 emerges, in print, on the Internet **2** objective of, reinforce **3** channel, believe in
4 differentiate, from **5** begins with, convey **6** struggle, credibility

Writing 5: Persuasive communication online

The language of advertising

1
1 pushes the … button **2** titled **3** buy into **4** plenty of **5** fulfil

Changing features into benefits

1
1 giving you **2** which means **3** so you will be able to **4** which allows you to
5 meaning **6** which gives you

2
1 have,   which allow your   **2** has,   which means   **3** has,   giving you
4 have,   so you will be able to   **5** has,   which gives you
6 meaning

11 Accounting

Vocabulary: Key financial terms

1
1 direct **2** indirect **3** variable **4** fixed **5** overheads

2
A direct costs: 1 (example)   **C variable costs:** 1 (example), 3
B indirect costs: 2, 3, 4, 5   **D fixed costs:** 2, 4, 5

Vocabulary: Different types of cost

1
1 interest **2** maintenance **3** depreciation **4** navigation **5** catering
6 insurance

2
1 maintenance **2** insurance **3** navigation **4** interest **5** depreciation
6 catering

3
1 b **2** c **3** a
a 1 (example) **b** 3 **c** 1 **d** 2 **e** 1 **f** 3 **g** 2 **h** 1

Grammar: Gerunds

1
1 kept on buying , problem in sourcing **2** focus on keeping
3 interested in learning, experience of managing **4** good at troubleshooting ,
as a result of spending **5** challenge of getting

2
1 As a result of introducing the new system we've made significant cost savings.
2 Unfortunately, he's not very good at handling criticism.
3 The company doesn't have any problems in retaining staff.
4 We need to focus on getting a clear message across to consumers.
5 If we can keep on working at this rate we'll easily finish on time.

3
1 Travelling around the city by public transport is easy.
2 Installing the new computer system is going to be a slow process.
3 Sending out a questionnaire to all our customers is the first stage in the process.
4 Finding out everyone's requirements is essential before we start.
5 Studying and working at the same time isn't very effective.

4
1 on integrating **2** of becoming **3** in recruiting **4** in buying **5** of targeting

Skills: Polite language

1
1 d **2** e **3** a **4** c **5** b **6** e **7** f **8** d

2
1 B **2** B **3** A **4** A **5** A **6** B **7** A **8** B

3
1 have done a great job keeping **2** we really appreciate all your
3 it was nothing really **4** you made it look so easy **5** I'm afraid we missed
6 What we'd like to find out now
a 4 **b** 1 **c** 3 **d** 5 **e** 6 **f** 2

12 Microfinance

Vocabulary: Word formations

1
1 payee **2** penalty **3** guarantee **4** incentive **5** repay **6** sustainable
7 penalise

2
1 penalise **2** incentivise **3** repayment **4** guarantor **5** penalty **6** payee

Vocabulary: Strategies for understanding unknown words

1
1 B 2 C 3 B 4 A 5 A 6 C 7 B 8 A 9 B 10 C

2
1 penalty *penalise* 2 in *on* 3 entries *entities* 4 require *requirements*
5 guarantee *guarantor* 6 sustainability *sustainably*

Grammar: *Used to, be used to* and *get used to*

1
Active verb: 4, 6
Passive verb: 1, 5
Adjective: 2, 3

2
1 f 2 d 3 h 4 g 5 c 6 b 7 e 8 a

3
1 will get used to driving 2 used to have 3 get used to working
4 got used to using 5 used to find, am used / am getting used to finding
6 not used to commuting 7 am used to having 8 will be used to working
9 has been used to starting / has got used to starting 10 used to buy

Skills: Use techniques to improve your delivery (stress, chunking and pace)

1
1 First of all | I'd like to thank you all for coming today | – it's great to see so many people.
2 So | who are we | and what do we do?
3 We aim to extend credit to some of the world's poorest people | to help them to help themselves.
4 Unlike a traditional bank | we will visit our customers | – we don't expect them to come to us.
5 And | there are no charges for late payments | and no minimum loan amount.
6 That means anyone | at any level | can get credit from us.

2
This is your victory. | I know you didn't do this | just to win an election | and I know you didn't do it for me. | You did it because you understand the enormity of the task that lies ahead.| For even as we celebrate tonight, | we know the challenges that tomorrow will bring | are the greatest of our lifetime – two wars, | a planet in peril, | the worst financial crisis in a century.

3
1 conventional 2 more 3 reversed 4 attractive 5 collateral 6 loan
7 guarantee
The conventional banks are based on one basic principle: | the more you have, | the more you can get.
We reversed that principle. | Our principle is this | – the less you have, | the more attractive you are for us.
In order to create a completely new bank, | we have to get rid of the whole idea of collateral.
We said | I don't need anything, | I'll just give you a loan.
And that's what we do. | We have no collateral. | We have no guarantee.

Reading 6 Microfinance for small business owners

1
1 they can't get credit from the banks 2 Self-employed people
3 find it difficult to raise capital for larger loans. 4 they had a cash-flow problem.
5 complex 6 they do not normally lend such large amounts.

2
1 c 2 d 3 f 4 e 5 a 6 b

3
1 to get back on their feet 2 sitting on 3 turned down
4 the hoops we had to go through

4
1 d 2 f 3 g 4 a 5 c 6 e 7 b

5
1 readily associated, turned down 2 deprived, get back on their feet 3 encounter, conduct due diligence 4 increasingly common, raise finance 5 sitting on, downtime 6 meet, demand, constraints 7 five-figure sum

Writing 6: Formal and informal emails at work

Formality and functions

1
1 carbon copy 2 that is 3 regarding 4 as soon as possible 5 by the way
6 for your information 7 please 8 laugh out loud

2
Formal: 1, 2, 3, 6   Informal: 3, 4, 5, 6, 7, 8

Functions of emails

1
a **informing** 2, 6 b **inviting** 8 c **requesting** 5, 9, 10 d **thanking** 1, 7
e **confirming** 2, 4, 6 f **apologising** 3 g **developing a relationship** 1, 4

2
a **colleague to colleague, informal** 2, 5, 7, 9 b **client to supplier /supplier to client, formal** 1, 3, 4, 8, 10 c **colleague to colleague, formal** 6

13 Corporate Social Responsibility

Vocabulary: CSR topic vocabulary

1
1 compelled 2 deception 3 well-being 4 generated 5 bluffing 6 vast

2
1 c 2 d 3 e 4 a 5 b

3
1 vast 2 primary purpose 3 stakeholders 4 bluffing 5 box-ticking exercise
6 well-being 7 work-life balance 8 Procurement policies 9 generate
10 compelled 11 deceive

Grammar: Phrases with prepositions

1
1 of 2 of 3 on 4 on 5 within 6 into 7 at 8 in 9 of

2
a 3, 5, 6, 7 b 1, 4 c 2, 8, 9

3
1 by *within* 2 set *setting* 3 to *on* 4 working *work* 5 to *at* 6 within *into*
7 about *of* 8 transparency *transparent* 9 on *of*

4
1 B 2 C 3 B 4 A 5 C 6 A 7 C 8 B 9 B

Skills: Supporting the speaker through listener responses

1
1 Uh-huh. Sure 2 Hmm, maybe. 3 Good. Yes. Absolutely 4 Oh 5 [silence]
6 Uh-huh 7 Great 8 Yes, really

2
Positive: 1, 3, 7, 8 **Negative:** 4, 5 **Neutral:** 2, 6

3
1 Oh [falling or flat intonation] 2 Hmm [flat intonation]
4 Maybe [falling or flat intonation] 5 Uh-huh [flat intonation]
1 c 2 b 3 b 4 a 5 c

14 Strategic planning

Vocabulary: Verbs for strategic planning

1
1 conducting **2** consult **3** implement **4** specify **5** monitor **6** deviate
7 Ensuring
2
1 specify *implement* **2** develop *monitor* **3** consult *conduct*
4 implement *develop* **5** conduct *deviate* **6** implement *ensure* **7** ensure *consult*
3
1 A **2** C **3** A **4** B **5** A **6** C **7** C **8** B **9** B

Vocabulary: Multi-word verbs and collocations

1
1 on with **2** over **3** away with **4** up against **5** across **6** through **7** off
8 up with **9** across **10** on **11** up **12** over
2
1 c **2** e **3** b **4** f **5** g **6** a **7** h **8** d
3
1 up **2** away with **3** across **4** on **5** through **6** over **7** off **8** up
9 up against **10** on

Skills: Narrative tenses

1
1 was working **2** had gone **3** was checking **4** walk
5 had been **6** didn't dare **7** called **8** shouts
Past simple: 6, 7   **Past perfect:** 2, 5   **Past continuous:** 1, 3   **Historic present:** 4, 8
2
1 was coming **2** had **3** had left **4** say **5** asked
6 had ordered **7** were coming **8** (had) changed

Skills: Answering questions in interviews

1
1 c **2** b **3** a
2
1 were still doing   didn't see
2 were having   forgotten   see
3 had never worked   organised

Reading 7 Henry Mintzberg

1
1 d **2** e **3** g/a **4** a/g **5** b **6** c **7** f
2
1 F **2** T **3** T **4** F **5** F **6** F
3
Sentence b best summarises the sentence from the text.
4
1 renowned **2** prolifically **3** prestigious **4** over-zealous **5** influential
6 prominent **7** novel
5
1 d **2** b **3** a **4** e **5** c
a defines *take apart* and b defines *single out*
6
1 renowned, prestigious **2** earning, influential **3** novel, made, contribution
4 singled out, took on **5** over-zealous, took apart

Writing 7: First contact emails

Analysing emails

1
1 b **2** c **3** a **4** a
1 F **2** F **3** I **4** F
1 respectful, divergent, indirect
2 respectful, convergent, direct
3 friendly, convergent, direct
4 respectful, divergent, direct

Tone through word choice

1
1 F **2** F **3** I **4** I
2
1 e **2** f **3** a **4** c **5** d **6** b
3
3, 1, 4, 2, 6, 5

Progress test 1: Units 1–5

1
1 set up **2** was selling **3** decided **4** had won **5** launched **6** had reached
7 was working **8** took over **9** have held **10** has grown
2
1 We will definitely need to make the environment a priority.
2 I suppose we might have more 'virtual' offices.
3 We may even stop business trips and only use teleconferencing.
4 We are certainly going to develop markets in Africa and India.
5 The Eurozone might well extend further.
6 I think it must have crashed.
7 We should have asked for extra time in the last meeting.
8 He might have gone to the dentist.
3
1 cash flow **2** retention rates **3** shareholder value **4** programme
5 goals **6** incentives **7** profit **8** equity-based
4
1 Can/Could I ask **2** are you? **3** Why don't we
5
1 creativity **2** Implement **3** atmosphere **4** personality **5** package
6 incentives **7** performance **8** innovation **9** interaction **10** convergence
11 budget **12** department
6
1 largely monopolised **2** acted illegally **3** heavily regulated
4 increasingly globalised **5** invested heavily **6** organisational
7 reconsidering **8** genetically modified
7
1 pay *payment* **2** wage *salary* **3** expensive *expense* **4** organical *organic*
5 monopoly *oligopoly*

Progress test 2: Units 6–10

1
1 apologise **2** thank **3** deny **4** offer **5** agree **6** promise
7 apologised for being **8** thanked (me) for helping **9** denied putting
10 offered to help **11** agreed to send **12** promised to give
2
1 have/'ve been **2** have/'ve been meeting **3** (have been) getting
4 Have (you) been working **5** have/'ve just started **6** will/'ll be visiting
7 will/'ll be spending **8** will/'ll have completed **9** will not/won't be finished
3
1 had been, wouldn't have to **2** wouldn't have made, hadn't gone
3 won't be able, completes **4** had bought, wouldn't be
5 would never have agreed, had realised **6** had fixed, wouldn't have had
4
1 should have set **2** might have won **3** could have spent **4** might not have built
5
1 out **2** out **3** into **4** of **5** to **6** into
6
1 stand, of **2** give, to **3** avoid, between **4** create, between **5** enhance, in
6 explore, for
7
1 undertake, gather **2** pilot, tackle **3** rapport, However **4** boost, slash
8
1 outlets, store **2** retailer, consumers **3** media, mix **4** marketing
9
1 awareness, perceptions **2** iconic, extensions **3** optimisation,
relationship **4** transparency, uncomplicated **5** inspirational, affordable

Progress test 3: Units 11–14

1

*[Note: other prepositions are possible with some of these nouns (e.g. experience **in** or method* **for***) but these answers reflect the expressions which are presented in the SB]*

1 for   **2** of   **3** of   **4** of   **5** in   **6** of   **7** on   **8** at

2

1 Listening, is the most   **2** Ensuring, is our main   **3** Commuting, is stressful

3

1 was used to, get used to   **2** didn't use to, am not used to
3 used to, 'm getting used

4

1 d   **2** f   **3** a   **4** e   **5** b   **6** c

5

1 conscious of the risks   **2** be transparent in their procedures   **3** look at costs
4 be integrated into the system   **5** have an impact on the situation
6 amount of interest

6

1 stayed   **2** had booked   **3** was visiting   **4** had had   **5** says / said   **6** was sitting
7 had told   **8** hadn't had   **9** wasn't waiting   **10** left

7

1 maintenance   **2** incentivise   **3** navigation   **4** sustainably   **5** capitalise
6 depreciation   **7** penalise   **8** guarantor   **9** payee   **10** repayments

8

1 work-life balance   **2** come up with ideas   **3** procurement policies
4 move forward   **5** population density   **6** box-ticking exercise   **7** into practice
8 take time over the decision

9

1 consult   **2** evaluate   **3** specify   **4** develop   **5** implement   **6** monitor
7 ensure   **8** deviate

10

1 put up with   **2** took off   **3** put (it) off   **4** took over   **5** put down
6 come through

Acknowledgements

The authors and publishers acknowledge the following sources of copyright material and are grateful for the permissions granted. While every effort has been made, it has not always been possible to identify the sources of all the material used, or to trace all copyright holders. If any omissions are brought to our notice, we will be happy to include the appropriate acknowledgements on reprinting.

Chillibreeze for the text on p. 12 © The copyright of this material is owned by Chillibreeze Solutions Pvt Ltd (www.chillibreeze.com), an India based company providing content and design services to clients across the globe. Being used with permission;

The Sunday Times for the article on p. 21 'Entrepreneurs – born or made?' by Rachel Bridge, *Sunday Times* 4 July 2010 © Rachel Bridge / The Sunday Times / NI Syndication;

A & C Black for the text on p. 30 & 48 taken from *Business: The Ultimate Resource* © A&C Black, a member of the Bloomsbury Group, 2006;

Harvard Business Review for the article on p. 39. Reprinted by permission of *Harvard Business*, 'What would Peter say?' by Rosabeth Moss Kanter, November 2009. Copyright © 2009 by the Harvard Business School Publishing Corporation; all rights reserved;

The Financial Times for the article on p. 57 'Microfinance sees demand leap' by Jonathan Moules, *Financial Times* 12 September 2010 © Financial Times Ltd, 2010;

Henry Mintzberg for the text on p. 66 'Henry Mintzberg: Strategy Guru'. Reproduced with permission of Henry Mintzberg.

Development of this publication has made use of the Cambridge English Corpus (CEC). The CEC is a computer database of contemporary spoken and written English, which currently stands at over one billion words. It includes British English, American English and other varieties of English. It also includes the Cambridge Learner Corpus, developed in collaboration with the University of Cambridge ESOL Examinations. Cambridge University Press has built up the CEC to provide evidence about language use that helps to produce better language teaching materials.

The publishers are grateful to the following for permission to reproduce copyright photographs and material:

Key: l = left, c = centre, r = right, t = top, b = bottom

Alamy /©Keith Morris for p. 13(tl & tr), /©John Angerson for p. 13(bl), /©Global Warming Images for p. 13(br); Courtesy of Innocent Drinks for p. 47; iStockphoto /©Jon Schulte for p. 65; Photolibrary.com /©Robert Harding Travel for p. 12, /©Imagebroker RF for p. 20, /©Image 100 for p. 29 & p. 30, /©Jose Luis Pelaez Inc for p. 38; Rex Features /©Sipa Press for p. 11; Courtesy of Steve Raftery, Sky-Garden.co.uk for p. 56

Cover photo: Shutterstock /©Leung Cho Pan

Photos sourced by: Suzanne Williams/Pictureresearch.co.uk

Proofreader: Marcus Fletcher

The publisher has used its best endeavours to ensure that the URLs for external websites referred to in this book are correct and active at the time of going to press. However, the publisher has no responsibility for the websites and can make no guarantee that a site will remain live or that the content is or will remain appropriate.